D1084544

NEW MAHĀYĀNA

Buddhism for
a Post-Modern World

AKIZUKI Ryōmin

TRANSLATED BY

James W. Heisig & Paul L. Swanson

ASIAN HUMANITIES PRESS
Berkeley, California

ASIAN HUMANITIES PRESS

Asian Humanities Press offers to the specialist and the
general reader alike the best in new translations of major
works and significant original contributions to our understanding of Asian religions, cultures, and philosophies.

"Asian Humanities Press" is a trademark of
Jain Publishing Company.

ISBN 0-89581-900-7
LCCCN 90-83802

Printed in the United States of America

CONTENTS

Translators' Introduction

In September of 1959, *Newsweek* ran an article about a young Zen monk in Japan calling for a radical reform of Buddhism. "I want to help revive the real spirit of Zen," announced the 38-year-old Akizuki Ryōmin. "To do so, we must break the formalism that constricts Zen and expose the false masters."[1] Encouraged by D. T. Suzuki's dark appraisal of the state of Zen in Japan at the time, and also by the passionate call of Shaku Jōkō, one of the leading figures in the world of Zen at the time, to "kill all the priests and burn all the temples in order to bring Zen back to life," Akizuki threatened to begin shaking the tradition out of its lethargy by publishing the secret answers to hundreds of the classical kōan.

He did not in fact go through with his threat,[2] but he did devote the next thirty years to thinking and writing about his revolution, culminating in his proclamation of a "New Mahāyāna." The book that bears that title and is presented here in translation, is the first of Akizuki's works to appear in English.[3]

---

[1] "The Real Spirit of Zen?", *Newsweek* (21 September 1959): 121–22. The article was based on an interview with the Tokyo-based journalist A. W. Jessup.

[2] Akizuki does reveal one such "secret answer" (see below, 63 and n. 6). But already in 1916, well before Akizuki had leveled his threat, an unauthorized publication of kōan answers had appeared in Japanese under the title 現代相似禅の評論 [*A Critique of Present-day Pseudo-Zen*], and caused a sensation. It was later translated and published in English by Yoel Hoffmann under the title *The Sound of the One Hand: 281 Zen Koans with Answers* (Paladin: 1977).

[3] 秋月龍珉, 新大乗 — 仏教のポスト・モダン (Tokyo: Suzuki Shuppan, 1988).

A Zen Master in the Rinzai tradition, Akizuki is a revolutionary whose target is the self-understanding of Buddhist faith in the contemporary world and whose principal weapon is the written word. He has no temple of his own and no officially certified line of disciples, nor does he seem the least bit interested in locking horns with the Buddhist hierarchy and establishment as such. He has never had a tenured university position until this year, when he was offered a professorship at Hanazono University in Kyoto. Simply put, the focus of his revolution is the modes of thought that govern the way Buddhist priests today — and Zen monks in particular — locate themselves in society and interpret the experience of enlightenment. Instead of seeking the reform of particular structures, he navigates his way in and out of the system in order to foster what he, in the best Zen tradition, considers the only lasting reform: the awakening of the individual self.

That Akizuki has found an audience for his ideas in the Japanese-speaking world is an understatement. His 15 volumes of *Collected Writings* and over 30 other books have made his name known far and wide. He has a record 6 titles published in Kōdansha Shinsho and the same number again in PHP Bunko, two of the most highly respected and best-selling series of high-level popularizations in all of Japan. In addition, he edits a monthly journal entitled *Mahāyāna Zen*.[4]

Given the fact that the vast majority of the output of Japanese academics have to put up with a pitifully small readership and virtually no tradition of critical reviewing, it comes as little surprise that writers who find a way to bring the results of the scholars' efforts to the public eye and stir up controversy should raise so many eyebrows. This is no less true in Akizuki's case. But if he has not sought a career in the world of Buddhist scholars, he has kept up constant ties with that world and is remarkably *au courant* of research going on.

---

[4] 大乗禅 . For the past several years, the journal has published the papers of the annual conference of the Japan Chapter of the Society for Buddhist-Christian Studies in a special double-issue.

What is more, far from shying away from the critical attention of Buddhist scholars, he seems to thrive on it.

Akizuki's medicine is not always easy to swallow. There are times when one disagrees with the diagnosis, and times when one would prefer another prescription than the one he gives. There are even times when one might wish for an antidote to the doctor himself. Whether one reads Akizuki's writings as a scholar, a simple believer, or merely someone interested in Japanese Buddhism, there is something in them to annoy everyone.

At the same time, the state of Buddhism in Japan as he reflects it — even when refracted in his own idiosyncratic way — is too obvious to ignore. The proliferation of "new religions" in Japan, based on traditional Buddhism but breaking with the inherited structures, are evidence enough of just how widespread the need for change is felt today. Add to that the growing number of Buddhist communities seeking to enter into dialogue with other religions and face the problems of science and technology head on, and Akizuki's New Mahā-yāna movement cannot but touch home.

All the same, there is bound to be a great deal here sure to surprise the general Western readership interested in Zen Buddhism. For those in the West who have tended to think of Zen as a mere meditative technique of use to them in their own faith, as a religious tradition relatively detached from the concrete culture and history of the people who practice it, or a noble theory that casts none of the institutional shadows of Christendom, Akizuki offers good tonic. Something Rudolf Otto wrote in 1930 comes to mind here:

> When one compares two religions or confessions with one another, he ought to avoid the mistake which Harnack points out when he warns against comparing "one's own good theory with the other's bad practice," one's own ideal with the mere reality of the other. One must be as just at this point as is possible, must compare theory with theory, ideal with ideal, and, if he wishes to be absolutely just, he must not content himself with the view of the religion gained from the life of even its best representatives, but with that which

would be gained if it should be really lived according to its last and best ideals. The religion under consideration has also the right to demand that one should not measure or evaluate it according to incidental, mere peripheral traits and conditions, which have always clung to it, and still cling, but could be eliminated without altering its essential character.[5]

One cannot read Akizuki without feeling that he has taken the same warning to heart. The portrait of Buddhism he paints in this book, even though it was intended for a Japanese Buddhist audience, seeks a great harmony between theory and practice, and at no point falls into the familiar trap of using Buddhist ideals to censure Christian practice. But not only that. He tries to show how the breakdown of this harmony in the actual lived reality of Japanese Buddhism has turned around to affect the way the ideals themselves are understood. This is why he insists that his "revolution" is primarily a "restoration." For Akizuki, the historical figure of Śākyamuni and the spirit of the founders of sectarian Buddhism offer a kind of permanent protestant principle to call our current practice and self-understanding to task.

As revolutions in Buddhism go, Akizuki's is not without precedence. Insofar as it embraces both scholarship and popular belief, it is in the tradition of Ikkū and Bankei—steeped in the texts, sayings, and methods of the past, yet iconoclastic with regard to institutional rigor mortis and oppressive social customs. He follows Shinran's lead in focussing on a lay Buddhism, and his tone is at times reminiscent of Nichiren's prophetic call for reform. Yet he has given little attention to structuring his own New Mahāyāna into a durable institution on its own, preferring, he says, to leave this to the younger generation of Buddhists.[6]

---

[5] Cited in the English translation by F. H. Foster, *India's Religion of Grace and Christianity Compared and Contrasted* (London: SCM Press, 1930), 59.

[6] See 対話「新大乗」 [*A Dialogue on "New Mahāyāna"*] (Tokyo: Suzuki Shuppansha, 1989), 78.

Regarding his relations with Christianity, Akizuki has never shied away from stating the importance he gives to Jesus, whom he has called "the supreme practicer of Zen,"[7] elevating him even above Bodhidharma in importance for the contemporary Zen Buddhist.[8] At the same time, he finds the standpoint of universalism, whether of a Christian or Buddhist stamp, to be an idea that has outlived its time. More particularly, he attributes the desire to encompass all believers within a single religious tradition as an expression of a dangerous tendency deeply rooted in the Japanese psyche and inimical to true religious belief.[9] For the same reason, both in personal life and in his New Mahāyāna, Akizuki has tried to steer away from political establishments of all sorts. Any kind of association of Japanese patriotism with religion he abhors.[10]

In preparing this book for translation, a certain amount of editing and abridgement has been done to eliminate repetition. It was felt that Akizuki's circuitous, spiralling style of writing, if left to its own, would grate on the nerves of the English reader and interfere with the content. In all of this, we have tried to maintain his blend of the humorous and the chatty with the highly technical and dense. A large number of technical allusions have been tracked down and included in notes not in the original text. Japanese names have been identified by their Chinese characters on first appearance and, if not otherwise identified in the text, by a brief word about them. In this regard, we would like to acknowledge the gracious assistance not only of Akizuki Rōshi himself, but of his loyal assistant of some thirteen years, Kojima Masayo.

---

[7] See *Dialogue*, 60.

[8] The comment was made during a colloquium at the Nanzan Institute for Religion and Culture in May of 1990.

[9] The point is made in a discussion with Kubo Tsugunari 久保継成 , founder of the Reiyūkai, one of Japan's new postwar religions. See *Dialogue*, 338-39.

[10] In a somewhat rare published comment in this regard, he singles out the Sōka Gakkai's former policy of *kokuritsukaidan* and the Yasukuni shrine problem. See *Dialogue*, 333-34.

But these flourishes are all cosmetic. There is nothing in Akizuki's personality or his prose that gives the translator any leeway for pulling punches. As a writer who exempts no one from criticism by virtue of rank or personal relationship, he naturally divides the world around him wherever he treads. If anything, he welcomes just this sort of confrontation in the best thundering-and-thrashing style of Rinzai Zen. If we have been able to preserve something of this flavor, then the modest efforts that went into this translation will more than have had their reward.

James W. Heisig
Paul L. Swanson

Nanzan Institute for Religion and Culture
Nagoya, Japan
1 June 1990

Foreword

In this book I am advocating a "New Mahāyāna" Buddhism. The material that makes it up is drawn mainly from talks and writings of the past several years, brought together and published here for the first time, but the story behind it goes back a good deal further than that.

As a young man I came into contact with a Christian teacher — stern as an old samurai, he was — and entered the Protestant faith. In later years my eyes were opened to the faith of Shinran and I made an about-face in the direction of Pure Land Buddhism, the tradition to which my family belonged. Only after that did I come to know the enchantment of Zen. For all the vicissitudes of my youth, a single desire prevailed above all: the desire to be enlightened. With the aid of the right master, I finally reached my goal and attained an experience of enlightenment about half the size of the hindquarters of a flea.

I also spent a number of years of my youth studying in the borderlands between religion and philosophy until, with the help of Nishida Kitarō's idea of "the locus of inverse correspondence,"[1] I was able to bring my ideas to a provisional conclusion and write them up into an undergraduate thesis for the Department of Philosophy of Tokyo University. Suzuki Daisetz, who was living in the United

---

[1] The notion of "the locus of inverse correspondence" (場所的逆対応) as developed in the thought of Nishida Kitarō (1870-1945), Japan's first great modern philosopher, is fundamentally an attempt to incorporate the element of self-transformation into a logic of dialectical opposition.

States at the time, was kind enough to send me a small subsidy to encourage me to pursue my research and to publish my work, immature though it was. But my mind was on other things. My first duty, I felt, was to immerse myself in Zen, to become "one who has completed the Great Matter," that is, one who has gone through Hakuin's systematic discipline of the *kōan*.[2] There would be time for the rest later. I requested permission of Suzuki Sensei to use the money to further my Zen practice and he kindly gave his consent.

And so it was that I set out on a search of a meditation hall where I might practice every day. In no time I found myself knocking at the gates of the Musashino Prajñā Meditation Hall, which I had heard about from Itō Kōan Sensei,[3] a former professor from my days at Waseda University. There I met with Osaka Kōryū Rōkan[4] and for the first time heard the term "New Mahāyāna." That was more than thirty years ago.

Already prior to that time I had practiced Zen under experienced masters — before the war, Miyata Tōmin Rōshi, and after the war, Furukawa Gyōdō Sensei,[5] to whom I had been introduced by Daisetz Sensei. Later I practiced meditation from dawn to dusk at a site known as Prajñā Cave. It was there that I completed Rinzai Zen's "Great Matter." I then went on to practice under Ōmori Sōgen

---

[2] Hakuin Ekaku 白隠慧鶴 (1686-1769) revitalized the Rinzai process of meditating on kōan during the modern period, and his teachings became the central Rinzai tradition in Japan. All modern Rinzai masters trace their lineage to Hakuin.

[3] Itō Kōan 伊藤康安 is Professor Emeritus of Japanese Literature and Philosophy at Waseda University and a priest of Shun'u-ji.

[4] Osaka Kōryū 苧坂光龍 was the second president of the Śākyamuni Association. Throughout the book, Akizuki uses different titles to indicate his relationship to people. *Sensei* 先生 is a general term for teachers or significant elders, *rōshi* 老師 is used by disciples in the Rinzai tradition to address their Zen masters, *rōkan* 老漢 refers to a teacher to whom one is particularly close, and *senji* refers to a deceased master.

[5] Miyata Tōmin 宮田東珉 was former superintendent of the Kenchō-ji branch of Rinzai; Furukawa Gyōdō 古川堯道 was former superintendent of the Enkaku-ji branch.

Rōshi of the "Tesshū Society."[6] Finally, at the age of reason at fifty, I was ordained a monk under Yamada Mumon Rōshi[7] and was inscribed in the monastic registers of the Myōshin-ji branch.

And so it is that I have passed my years until now as a scholar-monk, a teacher of Zen without a temple of his own. In addition to having served as a professor of philosophy and religion, I have published some 30 volumes of works on Zen Buddhism. Fully half of my life has been spent on the jeweled path[8] of the follower of Zen — as someone has said, "walking a path with the religious sandal of the Zen Way on one foot and the scholarly sandal of Zen studies on the other."

Through all of my comings and goings, a single thought has remained with me: "Is this enough for Buddhism?" It was a question I had picked up from the revolutionary religious thought of Shaku Jōkō Rōshi, the founder of the Prajñā Meditation Hall and "religious revolutionary of the Shōwa era."[9] In chapter 2 I shall touch on the ideas of Jōkō Rōshi, which I learned from Kōryū Rōkan. (Incidentally, the latter was himself a dyed-in-the-wool conservative, which confirmed in me the same sense of atavism I had had when I was doing meditation with Ōmori Rōshi and felt the strong, though indirect, influence of the religion of his master Seki Bokuō Rōshi.)[10] As we will see, for Jōkō Rōshi, the answer to the problem of how to bring the true spirit of Mahāyāna Buddhism to the modern world lay in "prajñā Buddha Dharma." As the last Japanese monk to hold on

[6] Ōmori Sōgen 大森曹玄 was former president of Hanazono University and head of the Tesshū Society 鉄舟会, a Zen society that he himself founded.

[7] Yamada Mumon 山田無文, former superintendent of the Myōshin-ji branch of Rinzai and president of Hanazono University, passed away in 1988 at the age of 88.

[8] Akizuki is punning on the unusual character 珉 in his own personal name, which means a kind of jewel.

[9] Shaku Jōkō 釈 定光 was the first president of the Śākyamuni Association. The Shōwa era began in 1925 and ended on January 7, 1989 with the death of Emperor Hirohito.

[10] Seki Bokuō 関 牧翁 was former superintendent of the Tenryū-ji branch of Rinzai.

to the *vinaya* precepts,[11] he came out in favor of "lay Buddhism" as the Buddha Dharma best suited to our times. I determined to make it my goal to carry on the line of religious reform initiated by Jōkō Rōshi.

Happily, there was another pioneer to help show me the way: Hisamatsu Shin'ichi Sensei, who referred to himself as a "post-modernist" and was proposing what he called "FAS Zen."[12] In addition, I had studied philosophy under Mutai Risaku Sensei[13] and later under Nishitani Keiji Sensei.[14] All of these elements fit together naturally to shape my idea of a "post-modern Buddhism" and to focus on the question: What does Buddhism, and in particular Zen Buddhism, have to say about facing up to modernity and overcoming it?

This was also the way Suzuki Daisetz Sensei had formulated the problem for "world Zen," a problem which he felt it impossible for Buddhist believers alive today to sidestep. The fact that one happens to be a person of little learning and altogether lacking in genius, immature and weak of virtue, is not sufficient reason to stand by idly and keep quiet. With this idea burning within me, I took up my pen to write this little book. One of those who read it in draft form wondered what kind of an audience it could possibly be aimed at. Is it for the specialist, he asked, or is it for the general public? I cannot even begin to answer that question myself. It has taken all

---

[11] The term is vague; it can refer either to one belonging to the Risshū sect (one of the six sects dating from the 8th century in Japan, it is based on the Dharmaguptạ precepts or *vinaya*), or to one who truly keeps the precepts of the *vinaya* in daily life. The context suggests the latter.

[12] The acronym in FAS Zen, a movement founded by Hisamatsu Shin'ichi 久松真一 , stands for Formless self, All humanity, and Superhistorical history. This is treated briefly in chapter 3 below, 44.

[13] Mutai Risaku 務台理作 was former president of Bunrika University, and a prominent disciple of Nishida Kitarō.

[14] Nishitani Keiji 西谷啓治 is professor emeritus of Kyoto University and a prominent disciple of Nishida Kitarō. In addition to the widely acclaimed work *Religion and Nothingness* (Berkeley: University of California Press, 1982), translations of his books on *Nishida Kitarō* and *The Self-Overcoming of Nihilism* are slated for publication in the near future.

the energy I could muster just to organize on paper the thoughts that have been pressing in upon me. Suffice it to say that I do not consider Mahāyāna something to be taken lightly. No doubt there be those among my readers who will sympathize with the movement for a "New Mahāyāna" and take this book in the spirit in which it was written. At least that is the belief that prompts me to publish it.

As a companion to these pages I plan shortly to publish the results of the past several years of work in a book entitled *Under the Standard of the New Mahāyāna.*[15] Not long thereafter I expect to see published a collection of critiques of my proposal for a "New Mahāyāna" by six ranking Buddhist scholars from Tokyo University, arranged in the form of a series of dialogues.[16] If there be other criticism, I welcome it heartily.

Mahāprajñāpāramitā!

Akizuki Ryōmin
18 April 1988
Sokuhi-An

---

[15] Published as 「新大乗」の旗のもとに (Osaka: Tōhō Shuppan, 1988).
[16] *A Dialogue on "New Mahāyāna"*, see above, x, n. 6.

The Call for a New Buddhism

1 The Prospects for a New Buddhism

WEDDINGS BUT NOT FUNERALS

I will never forget the first time I heard the words "New Mahāyāna." The day was February 4, 1951, and the occasion was my first formal interview with Osaka Kōryū Rōkan of the Prajñā Meditation Hall. He struck me as a man of about 50 years of age—very young to be a master, I remember feeling at the time, and I frankly wondered whether he would really do. Earlier I had had formal interviews with Gotō Zuigan Rōshi, Asahina Sōgen Rōshi, and then Shirōzu Keizan Rōshi,[1] all three of whom were too young for me to bring myself to practice under. Perhaps it was just the fact that all the rōshi I had met up until then were rather more elderly monks. In any case, at the time I was on the mailing list of those who received a small "Monthly Bulletin" from Kōryū Rōkan. There I ran across the words "New Mahāyāna," as well as a sentence which read: "Although I do perform weddings, I do not myself officiate at funerals." The words touched me to the quick and that very day I went to call on Kōryū

---

[1] Gotō Zuigan 後藤瑞巌 was superintendent of the Myōshin-ji and Daitoku-ji branches of Rinzai. Asahina Sōgen 朝比奈宗源 was superintendent of the Enkaku-ji branch of Rinzai. Shirōzu Keizan 白水敬山 was superintendent of the Heirin-ji branch of Rinzai.

Rōkan. Despite his youth, I felt that the words "New Mahāyāna" had struck a bond between the two of us.

Not too long ago, a group of five close friends who had entered Tokyo University together after the War decided to have a get-together. Since I had gone on for my studies at Tokyo University only after leaving Waseda University and having taught for a spell, I was older than the others. Still, all of us had celebrated the "turn of the calendar" that marks the completion of one's sixtieth birthday, and we could not help looking at one another and feeling, "Look what old men the lot of us have turned into!" As most of us had passed the age of retirement from teaching, our discussion turned less on what lay ahead than on what had gone before. At one point in the conversation, someone brought up my conspicuous absence from the funeral of one of our teachers.

"I mean, being a bonze and all, and not to go to the funeral of an honored teacher . . ."

"But it is really *because* I am a bonze," I replied, "that I did not attend."

"Still the same old cross-grained Akizuki, aren't you?" he retorted, and everyone laughed.

When you stop to think about it, no religious functionaries anywhere in the world are maligned as much as Japanese Buddhist monks are. Everyone believes it to be bad luck to meet a monk in his robes in the first three days of the New Year. And if a bonze wears his robes to a hospital to visit someone, they tell him, "Good monk, isn't it a little *early* for you to be here?" The Protestant pastor and Catholic priest are there with the faithful from the cradle to the grave, and the idea that their presence in the hospital might bring bad luck never crosses anyone's mind. Quite the contrary, having a minister present at the end is welcomed by Christian believers.

It is otherwise with the Buddhist monk. Since his only function is to take care of the dead, his figure at once stirs up ancient Shinto feelings of the "unclean." Upon returning home from a funeral service, for example, Japanese are accustomed to be given "cleansing" salt at the entrance to their house. Naturally the bonze does not put himself through this Shinto ritual and so from the standpoint of ordinary people is classed among the "unclean." I find such unfair treatment distasteful and try as far as possible to avoid attending funerals dressed in my robes. Even if I am the only one to do so, I dare say I find it a good thing that a monk refuses to attend the funeral of a departed teacher.

Even though I happen to be Japanese, I detest *matsuri*. From my childhood the absurdity of these village festivals made my marrow melt. The shouldered floats or *mikoshi* jostling through the streets interfered with the buses and forced passengers to get out and walk. Houses that did not show an interest in the groups of young people carrying the *mikoshi* around had their fences rammed when the troupe passed by. Such barbarities date from the time of the mountain monks of Hiei who, assuming the authority of some god or other, roamed around at night dressed in deliberately obscene attire. *Matsuri* are not for the cultured.

I realize that those words amount to blasphemy against the many wholesome Japanese festivals, and maybe I should just let my feelings pass as a matter of personal taste. I once took occasion to reflect on this attitude of mine towards *matsuri*. I concluded that it may have something to do with the culture shock I received the first time I attended a Protestant church service as a young man and was struck by the purity of the religious atmosphere. The impression has never left me.

Be that as it may, I dislike "funerals" in general. For a long time I had no desire to attend weddings either, but of late I have made efforts to do so. When invited, I always reply with the stipulation, "if it is all right to come in my robes." If the couple and their parents agree, I go. And if I am asked to give a brief congratulatory speech, as is the custom at such events, I try whenever possible to insert a remark about why I have worn my robes to such a festive occasion. (Almost without fail there are audible whisperings to be heard around the banquet hall, "Look at that, a bonze!") I try to explain that real Buddhism is a way of life to help people wake up to who they originally are and to live out of their true self, and that for a long time the Buddhism of Śākyamuni had nothing at all to do with services for the dead.[2] In this way, I use the wedding ceremony as an occasion to spread an understanding of Buddhism that might do something to alter the image people have of the monk.

TOKUGAWA FEUDALISM AND MONASTIC CORRUPTION

Why has the stature of today's Japanese Buddhist monk fallen as low as it has? A quick glance at history shows that the answer lies in the religious policy of Tokugawa feudalism. It is a matter of custom dating back no more than four hundred years.

Tokugawa Ieyasu, from the time he was a young landlord of Mikawa, was troubled by religious revolts.[3] When there was an outbreak at Mikawa, Ieyasu ordered the samurai generals to quell the disturbance, but since the samurai leaders were themselves devotees of the *nenbutsu* (the practice of reciting the name of Amida Buddha), they carried out the orders less than wholeheartedly. The attackers and the attacked merely went through the motions of a conflict, and there were even some among the lower-ranking samurai who ran over to the side of the rebels. Religion was a complicated affair, as Ieyasu was only too well aware from the successes and failures of his predecessors, Oda Nobunaga and Toyotomi Hideyoshi. Nevertheless, he was determined to use religion to his advantage. Drawing on the brains of Konchi-in Sūden and Tenkai Sōjō,[4] he undertook to work Buddhism into the funeral system.

---

[2] It is something of a cultural taboo in Japan to mention words of misfortune at wedding ceremonies, even in so indirect a fashion as to use terms homonymous with such words, such as the number 4 (pronounced *shi*, the same as the word for death) or 9 (pronounced *ku*, like the word for pain). Hence deliberate reference to death in a congratulatory speech is highly irregular.

[3] Tokugawa Ieyasu 徳川家康 was the founder of the Tokugawa Shogunate, that ruled Japan from 1603 to 1868.

[4] Sūden 崇伝 (1569–1633) was a Rinzai monk affiliated with the Konchi-in of Nanzen-ji. He was appointed by Ieyasu to be his counselor and given the responsibility of supervising all Buddhist institutions and formulating a decree against Christianity. Tenkai Sōjō 天海僧正 (1536–1643) was a Tendai monk and

The result was the firm establishment of the "temple registration" system peculiar to Japanese Buddhism. The people of Japan were obliged to register their families as Buddhist at one of the Buddhist temples. Families not doing so were considered to be Christian and liable to death at the stake. Thus the Buddhist temple came to serve as a registrar for the government and the monk became a kind of civil servant. This is the first element to be considered.

Secondly, each daimyō had district schools set up for the education of younger generations of the samurai. These schools were restricted to the sons and daughters of the clan. For the children of the farmers, artisans, and merchants who made up the lower social strata, temple grammar schools were established to teach reading, writing, and arithmetic. Thus the monks became not only government registrars but also grammar school principals.

Third come the funerals and memorial services. When Śākyamuni died, he told his followers, "You are *not* to come to my funeral. Everything will be duly taken care of by the king and by aristocrats among the lay believers. You need only preserve my teachings and live according to the Dharma."[5] And indeed for a long time in the Buddhist community of India, the monks lived with absolutely no connection to funeral rites. When Buddhism traveled to China by way of the Silk Road, it came under the cultural influence of Confucian thought, for which filial piety was one of the cardinal virtues and respect for ancestors a matter of great importance. What is more, the funeral was a major event for the Chinese, marking as it did the end of one's life.

In the course of acculturating itself to Chinese ways, Buddhism gradually came to foster respect for funerals and rites expressing fidelity to the ancestors, fashioning luxurious and ostentatious rituals

scholar who made the Tendai tradition a formidable presence in the Kantō area and is known for compiling the Tenkai edition of the Buddhist canon. Together, these two monks represent the most powerful Buddhist figures of their day.

[5] Akizuki's wording is a loose paraphrase of one of the many legends surrounding Śākyamuni's death.

of its own. It was this Chinese style of Buddhism that eventually found its way to Japan, whether by way of Korea or directly from China. Once there, it was taken up at first by the imperial court and nobility, but later spread to the common people.

The penetration of Buddhist funerals into Japanese culture at large may have been given added incentive by the native fear of *tatari*, or curses from the spirit world. Like all primitive peoples, the ancient Japanese lived in dread of the *tatari* of the dead. The extraordinary power of the Buddhist Dharma wielded by the monks was thought to be more powerful and effective than the powers of traditional Shinto for "calming the spirits." And so it was that a Japanese Buddhism centered on funerals and memorial services came to take root among the people.

I remember once visiting a temple when a young married woman came running through the vestibule of the main entrance, sobbing for help.

"My home is being hit by one misfortune after the other, and people tell me it is the *tatari* of the spirits of an ancestor whom we didn't hold a commemorative service for. Please come and say the prayers to calm the spirit. I beg you, please!"

On hearing this, the young monk blurted out angrily, "What kind of nonsense are you talking? Who has filled your head with such stupidities? Buddhism has nothing to do with such things."

But once he had regained his composure and was able to see that the poor woman was really at her wit's end, he softened his words. "All right, I will hold the service for you as you wish. Give me a call at your convenience." And with that he sent her on her way, greatly relieved.

The idea that the *tatari* of some departed ancestor or spirit is at work in a household where someone gets sick, where the husband's business collapses, and where a string of other calamities takes place promotes a religion of fear. Here we are at the end of the 20th century, in the midst of a scientific culture that enables us to fly people off the planet and leave footprints on the moon—and in Japan of all places, where the benefits of scientific technology are such as to rank us among the most highly developed nations on earth. And yet this kind of infantile belief in *tatari* is as alive and well now as it was in primitive societies of antiquity. What a strange country this is!

There are those who find it scandalous that sects calling themselves Buddhist should make the claim that "memorial services for the ancestors is the true heart of Buddhism." (Truth to tell, I myself once thought like this, but of late have come to think that services for the ancestors also belong to the story of the Japanese development of Mahāyāna Buddhism.) Śākyamuni himself, to put it bluntly, was atheistic and aspiritistic. He did not believe in the existence of gods or spirits or any Absolute outside of the self that controls the world and the people in it. To the question "Does the soul survive after death?" he could only reply, "No comment." For one who lives a full life, awakened to one's "original self" in the here and now, past and future are no longer an issue. But if the all-important *present self* is missing, some will-o-the-wisp or other is bound to slip in and take its place—call it God or Buddha or spirit or what you will. As I have often joked, "If parents are supposed to love their children, then we ought to sever ties with ancestors who come back to haunt their descendants." I realize this is somewhat mischievous on my part, but if no God or spirit outside of the self can be the Buddha Dharma of Śākyamuni, it is by no means unreasonable. The Buddha is neither outside of me nor inside of me; we cannot speak of the Buddha as being this or that. All right then, you might ask, where *is* the Buddha? Where is this "original self"? We will come to that question presently. For the moment, let us return to our point.

During the 300 years of the Tokugawa regime the monk, as a kind of civil servant functioning as a registrar and school principal, received allowances from the daimyō, the shogunate family, and the imperial palace. In addition, offerings were made by registered families at funerals and memorial services for the dead. Thus throughout the three centuries of the Tokugawa era, Buddhist monks not only forgot about expounding the teachings of Gautama Buddha, they forgot about what the founders of their own sects had taught. So comfortable was their social position within the feudal-clan system that Shin Buddhist monks no longer bothered with the teachings of Shinran, or Nichiren monks with the teachings of Nichiren.

With the Meiji Restoration and the opening of Japan, things changed. Registration was handed over to a village office and general education was transferred to the primary school system. What remained for the monks was only services for the dead — funerals and memorial services. This was the new context within which they were supposed to seek religious awakening. Actually, a small number of them did just that, returning to the teachings of their founders and spreading them with renewed zeal. But by and large, the monks spent their days in funeral services of one form or another.

This is pretty much the way things have remained up to the present. When there is a death in the family, the Japanese, even those who lead an all but religionless life, are almost certain to follow the customs of their *family* religion for the funeral. It is no less predictable that they will see to having memorial services performed for the ancestors. Thanks to these customs, the monks are able to make a living simply by performing services for the dead. This is why the "monk" has come to be thought of as a "master of ceremonies for the dead," and hence reduced to the pitiful status we now find him in. This is why the monk is viewed with special disdain in Japan.

For all that, the monk maintains a certain pride in himself as a "religious minister" and is grieved at the lack of respect his position is accorded in society at large. For ordinary people, the bonze is no more than an executor of rites for the dead, no different from those who work at the crematoria and funeral parlors. The three are all lumped together as playing roles related to death. Hardly anyone thinks of the monk as a religious minister in the same sense as a Protestant pastor or Catholic priest. The only difference between the monk and the undertaker or cremator is that the monk takes care of the *souls* of the ancestors. As for what is going on inside people at the time of these rituals, I am afraid it has nothing at all to do with Buddhism and is little more than a play of sentiments stemming from the same "fear of spirits" that has been part of the religious ignorance of the Japanese since primitive times. As Buddhists, monks

need to take a long, hard look at their situation and reawaken to a
sense of what it means to be a monk.

THE MONK AS OUTSIDER

The Buddhist temples and monks of today are altogether *within* society. Rather than expound the teachings of the Buddha and founders of their respective traditions, their days are spent in funerals and
memorial services. It is a criticism often heard, but for my part I see
some validity in what they are doing. Consider what happens when
a member of the family dies. If there were no funeral parlor operators
or crematorium staff prepared to take care of the dead, what would
ordinary people do? So, too, there is nothing untoward about having
monks administer the funeral rites and memorial services for the ancestors. What would we do without them? In offering this service,
temples and monks are playing an admirable role *within* society.
There is nothing disparaging about being called a "funeral monk,"
and no reason one should not take up the task with full confidence.

But if that is *all* there is, the social status of the monk is no different from those in the funeral business. It is mere wishful thinking to
imagine oneself as somehow "different" just because one is a monk.
For one thing, there is no higher and lower among occupations
within society. If the temple monk elects to assume the responsibilities of a "sacred minister" through the great rituals of human life associated with death, then he must make sure that he expounds the
Dharma (teachings) of the Buddhas and patriarchs. Only in so doing
can he rightly be called a Buddhist monk and "sacred minister." To
preach the Dharma is to show the way to people by criticizing society from *outside* society.

True enough, the *bhikku* who were the disciples of the Buddha
and took the path of homelessness were forbidden from having anything to do with funerals. For a long time, the *bhikku* who belonged
to the *saṅgha* (the community of monks who had left their homes for
a life of homelessness) in India had nothing to do with rites for the
dead. By taking their stand outside society, they cast in their lot with

the Dharma and through the Dharma criticized society, endeavoring to draw people to the Buddhist teachings. The monks of Japan today, in contrast, are simply a laity-called-monks. Theirs is a kind of "domesticated homelessness." If they are to call themselves monks and assume the responsibilities of "sacred ministers," then even if they have not left home *bodily*, they must do so in their *hearts*. They must be persons who have left the world — taken up a position *outside* society. They must in some sense take leave of the "law of the world" in order to be persons who live in the "law of Buddha." It is only from such a standpoint that they can preach the Dharma to society and show the way.

ARISE, NEW BUDDHISM! ROUSE YOURSELVES, MONKS!

Interest in Buddhism is growing stronger in the United States and Europe. Faced with this new challenge, it falls to the monks of Japan, as members of virtually the only remaining Mahāyāna Buddhist country, to rouse themselves as quickly as possible and devote themselves to the spread of the doctrines of their common religious leader, Śākyamuni, and of the founders of their respective sects. It is not a time to spend all one's energies in performing ceremonies for the dead.

Since the time of the Buddha, as we just noted, homelessness has always meant a life *outside* society, while the monks of today have landed themselves completely *within* society. Insofar as this represents one aspect of the whole of Mahāyāna, the roles they play within society are not altogether out of place. Quite the opposite, to commit oneself to live in the midst of the masses of the laity in order to bring them true salvation is to share in their sufferings, and that is surely part of the bodhisattva's way of "identification." Nevertheless, Buddhism issues a call to *the way of homelessness*. As one who answers this call, the monk must remain *outside* society, and not be so swallowed up *within* society that he forfeits a position from which to criticize society and guide it. Whether one happens to leave home bodily or not, without this basic homelessness of the heart one cannot be called a monk. In fact, one cannot even be called a Buddhist.

If monks today are to spread the teachings of their tradition, they need first to awaken to themselves as sacred ministers, to return to their founding fathers, and to appropriate their faith in their lives. This is the time and season that is upon us.[6] If the homelessness of the heart is not something reserved for the monks, neither is the need to awaken to true Buddhism. It applies as much to lay Buddhist believers. Indeed, to serve that cause is *the* Great Matter for the laity, and the monks — as laity-called-monks, the domesticated homeless.

Hence I have no mind to reject rites for the dead out of hand on the grounds that, as it is often put, "funerals serve no purpose and should be given up because all such rituals are without basis in original Buddhism." People may speak ill of "funeral bonzes," but it is often just such monks who have managed to keep up a poor country temple with no more than a few dozen homes on the registrar by teaching or working in a village office or a farming co-op. One should be careful of condemning too quickly. In my younger years I, too, embraced Shaku Jōkō Rōshi's uncompromising ideal of religious reform: "My heart's desire is to burn down every temple and kill every monk."[7] But as the years went by, I found myself wanting to join forces with the temples and monks to work for the reform of Buddhism — which was why I entered the monkhood. After all, even in its heyday, "Mahāyāna" Buddhism was a religious revival movement composed of a really small number of progressive homeless monks and a majority of lay believers.

Funerals are a solemn ritual marking the end of a human life. At

---

[6] Akizuki here uses the character for "autumn" and reads it "time" (which we have rendered "time and season"). He is playing here on the first character of his family name, which means literally "Autumn Moon."

[7] For details see 初めに大悲ありき [*In the Beginning Was the Great Compassion*], vol. 2 of 秋月龍珉著作集 [*Collected Writings of Akizuki Ryōmin*] (Tokyo: San'ichi Shobō, 1978).

such times, when people's hearts have been softened by pain and are ready for guidance, one should think not only of serving the dead but also of preaching the Dharma to those who have remained behind in life. Surely the helter-skelter of everyday life, in the midst of which one is apt to forget to commemorate the anniversary of an ancestor's passing, is nothing like a truly human life. And think of how difficult it must be for a family lodged in a modern apartment complex without so much as a Buddhist altar to see to the religious education of their children. In learning to see a particular meaning in each of the forms of religious *culture* left behind by former generations, I feel as if I have broken away from the narrow-minded puritanism of my youth.

As for me, I wish only to be remembered as a monk who went to weddings but not to funerals. I have no desire for a "funeral" after I die. I would simply ask that my immediate disciples and family lay me to rest with a chanting of the *Heart Sūtra* and the *Sankōryō*,[8] and a session of *zazen* for the time it takes to burn a single stick of incense. After what is of use in my body has been given to a medical university, let the rest be cremated. Rather than have my bones preserved, I would wish—like Hisamatsu Shin'ichi Sensei[9]—for them to be sunk to the bottom of the Akae Sea in my home town. If this be an offense against the civil laws governing burial, then perhaps there will be some way that even those bones could be useful to someone. It is very much a part of the Zen ideal for me that nothing be left behind, and I sincerely hope that my wishes will be carried out. With all my heart, I ask that I be allowed to end my life as a disciple of Zen in this way.

In the attempt to explain the call for a "New Mahāyāna," I have begun with a lament on the actual state of Buddhism in Japan and

---

[8] The *Heart Sūtra* (Prajñāpāramitā-hṛdaya-sūtra) is the shortest popular text in the voluminous Buddhist canon (only 260 Chinese characters in its most commonly used translation), and is often chanted in a variety of Buddhist ceremonies. The *Sankōryō* is explained in the following chapter.

[9] Hisamatsu's posthumous name, Hōseki Koji 抱石居士 , is used here.

its temples and monks. What I really have in mind, however, is a movement centered on reflective monks and enlisting kindred spirits from among the masses of laity. For such a movement to catch fire, monks will have to break free of the confinements that bind them in society at present — namely, their role as functionaries at Buddhist funerals and memorial services — and to reawaken to themselves as sacred ministers. They will have to recover the original sense of Buddhist homelessness and to take their stand as Mahāyāna bodhisattvas preaching the Dharma, as "the homeless of the heart outside society."

And just what is this "Dharma" they are to preach? It is, first of all, the radical recovery of and reeducation in Buddha Dharma as it was expounded by the founder of one's respective sect. From there, it is necessary to make one's way back again to the Buddha Dharma of Śākyamuni himself, so that the "one pure Buddha Dharma" can be preached from a firm grounding in one's own tradition. There is no other way to respond to what men and women today want from Buddhism. The time is now for a new Buddhism to emerge. This is what I mean by calling for a "New Mahāyāna."

Mahāprajñāpāramitā!

2 The Roots of the New Mahāyāna

RETURN TO ŚĀKYAMUNI

As I write these lines, it is January 1, 1988. In a mere 13 years we shall be into a new century. It has been 2,000 years since the Mahāyāna movement in Buddhism began and it seems to me just the right moment for a new Buddhism, a "New Mahāyāna," to rise up. But it is more than a matter of timing.

With the advance of scientific culture the world has become one. The very notion of a "human race," once no more than a bit of abstract common sense that people carried around in their heads, has in our own lifetime become a historical reality. Great superpowers like the United States and the Soviet Union can no longer take a step without taking into account the peoples of Asia and Africa. No country is exempt from the forces drawing the fate of the world together.

One can only stand in awe in the face of what modern civilization has managed to achieve. The secure position the modern idea of the "ego" has earned for itself has been another boon to humanity. At the same time, it is clear that the end of the modern world is upon us and that there is a need for a post-modern image of what it means to be human.

When we look at what Buddhism has been able to offer by way of an answer so far, we have to admit that it is time to initiate a movement for a new Buddhism. Where might such a movement begin? Where better than in a return to its founder, Śākyamuni. When people hear the injunction "Return to the Buddha!", their first thoughts go to "the early Buddhist canon" or to "primitive Buddhism." I mean to oppose these associations.

A highly respected scholar of primitive Buddhism once remarked that Buddhism came twice to Japan: first, in the time of Emperor Kinmei, when it was carried over to Japan by way of Korea; and second, during the Meiji period, when modern European Buddhist scholars introduced to Japan the scriptures of the *Nikāya* written in the sacred Pāli language of India. It was this second wave, he argued, that brought Japanese Buddhists in touch with the true teachings of the Buddha for the first time.[1]

This is a somewhat radical way of pointing to the culture shock the Japanese went through in suddenly being brought face to face with the reality of modern Europe. Up until the end of the Tokugawa era, Japan had known only the Chinese Buddhist scriptures, when out of nowhere they found themselves having to confront new Buddhist scholarship based on sūtras in an ancient Indian language and all decked out with the latest methodologies. Actually, the argument is a bit dated, as a closer look at the matter will show.

The so-called "primitive canon" that was transmitted to Sri Lanka does not as it is represent the "Buddha Dharma of Śākyamuni himself." The fact that it was transcribed in an ancient Indian language does not of itself permit the conclusion that it embodies the Buddhism of ancient times. The truth of the matter is, as scholars from Europe who have devoted themselves to a study of the question have stated time and again, the *Āgama* sūtras of the Chinese canon frequently attest to greater antiquity than the *Nikāya* of the Pāli scriptures, which, at least in their extant form, took shape only some

---

[1] The reference is to the Buddhist scholar Masutani Fumio, whose words are cited in note 3 of the following chapter. Incidentally, Masutani's *A Comparative Study of Buddhism and Christianity* (Tokyo: Young East Association, 1957) was one of the first of its kind by a Japanese scholar to appear in English.

five centuries into the Common Era. This being so, what can it possibly mean to speak of the Japanese coming to know the "true teachings of Śākyamuni" for the first time?

For people of a modern, rationalist frame of mind, Buddhism's so-called "primitive canon" (the *Nikāya* and *Āgama* sūtras) were extremely easy to understand. They picked out what they considered to be the true teachings of Śākyamuni, compared them to traditional "Mahāyāna doctrine," and rushed to the ludicrous conclusion that "Mahāyāna is not Buddhist doctrine."

I see two mistakes here. First, the fact that the *Nikāya* were written in an ancient Indian language came as such a dumbfounding discovery that they were directly assumed to be the *one and only* source material for information about the historical Śākyamuni. Second, the content of the texts of this "primitive canon" were read through the glasses of the modern European "ego." Claims that the "teachings of Śākyamuni" were being extracted from these texts were based entirely on the paltry brain-power of the scholars, while the "awe" that forms the cornerstone of true scholarship for a disciple of Buddhism was completely pushed aside. As Dōgen says, the Buddha Dharma is communicated "only between a Buddha and a Buddha."[2] I consider it a momentous oversight on the part of modern Buddhist studies originating in Europe to have forgotten this.

What is needed is to wipe the slate clean, to doff our modern rationalistic spectacles and set them to one side in order to have a second look at the "primitive canon." Only so can we help to shed new light on the teachings of "fundamental Buddhism" that form a continuous line with the tradition we have received from our forebears. "Only between a Buddha and a Buddha" means that only the enlightened Buddha can clearly perceive the true form of things or

---

[2] See the chapters of Dōgen's *Shōbōgenzō*, "Only between a Buddha and a Buddha" (唯仏与仏) and "A Dream Explained within a Dream" (夢中説夢). The phrase *only between a buddha and a buddha* comes originally from the beginning of the second chapter of the *Lotus Sūtra*, "On Expedient Means." See T 9.5c11 and Leon Hurvitz, *Scripture of the Lotus Blossom of the Fine Dharma* (New York: Columbia University Press, 1976), 22.

dharmaṣ. The scholarly intellectuals of contemporary Japan who hallow what has been extracted from the "primitive canon" as "the true teachings of Śākyamuni," have in reality fallen into an *avidyā*, the dark ignorance of the scholar who has forgotten what it means to treat one's subject matter with the requisite "awe." We must therefore take care to distinguish between what *they* call "primitive Buddhism" and the *true* "teachings of the Buddha." Hence I avoid the term "primitive Buddhism" and prefer to speak instead of "early Buddhism."

PRECANONICAL BUDDHISM

What I have been saying is nothing new. It has in fact been pointed out some time ago by a small number of thoughtful European scholars. The only ones who are likely to remain unaware of it are Japanese scholars who continue as before to lean heavily on foreign academics. I might mention, for example, the Polish scholar Stanislaus Schayer, who advanced the idea of a "precanonical Buddhism." The Buddhism that existed prior to the compilation of the teachings of Śākyamuni by the community of *bhikku*, he argued, rightly deserves the name of "early" (or "fundamental") Buddhism.

Surely this is common knowledge among Buddhist scholars today. The problem is to know just what this Buddhism means, and that in a sense much wider than simply what it happens to mean for scholars like Schayer. If the Buddha Dharma of Śākyamuni amounted to nothing more than the "Four Noble Truths, the twelvefold causal chain, and the Noble Eightfold Path," as scholars of "primitive Buddhism" claim, I can honestly say I would not find very much in Buddhism at all. Of all the innumerable teachings Śākyamuni expounded in response to lived situations, these may be the most crucial for the *bhikku* who leave home to form a community of disciples and walk together the Buddhist path of homelessness as Śākyamuni himself had. But even so, they are no more than *one form* of the Buddha Dharma, and we need to recognize that fact clearly.

For a hundred years after the death of Śākyamuni, the teachings of Buddhism are thought to have consisted mainly of the teachings of Śākyamuni himself. This is the period known as "early Buddhism." But once the first century had passed, a split developed between the Sthāvira conservatives and the more progressive Mahāsaṃghika school. Once this basic *radical* split was in place, the Buddhist tradition went through a series of *ramifying* splits, ushering in the age of "sectarian Buddhism." The *Nikāya* that survives to this day in Sri Lanka represents the transmission of one of twenty such sects, the Southern Theravāda. The Chinese texts of the *Agon* sūtras, meanwhile, represent the transmission of the Sarvāstivāda and two or three other sects. No doubt all of these are valuable texts in their own right, but care should be taken not to idolize them.

The claim of Schayer and other contemporary scholars that there is a pre-scriptural Buddhism is based on the idea that prior to the establishment of canonical Buddhism, the *bhikku* of early Buddhism organized the teachings of the Buddha and compiled them into "sūtras," which then finally became the "scriptures" of the various sects; and that in the process of systematizing the various theories, certain parts of the teachings of the Buddha were excised. I myself believe that truly important things were in fact left out in the process of compilation, and further that it was the aim of the "*prajñā* Buddha Dharma" of Mahāyāna, culminating in the figure of Nāgārjuna, to restore what had been lost.

The term *prajñā* is itself a case in point. Although it is generally thought to have come into use only after the emergence of Mahāyāna Buddhism, an important essay by Nishi Giyū[3] has demonstrated convincingly that the word was already in use early during the lifetime of Śākyamuni and was used to mean "original purity of mind." This would give the word *prajñāpāramitā* the sense of "perfection" (*pāramitā*) of "purity" (that is, of what is *śūnya* or empty). The idea of "original purity" that Nishi refers to also appears to have been ac-

---

[3] Nishi Giyū 西 義雄 is professor emeritus of Tōyō University. This reference is to his book 原始仏教に於ける般若の研究 [*Studies on "Prajñā" in Primitive Buddhism*] (Ōkurayama Seishin Kenkyūjo, 1953).

corded the authority of a teaching of the Buddha himself in the scriptures of the early period. But once the teachings of the Buddha had been systematized in the dogmatics of the Sthāvira current of "sectarian Buddhism," the idea ceased to be classified as part of the "vital core of Buddhism" and only scattered references were left throughout the "primitive canon." The prime importance of the idea of original purity found its way back into Buddhist doctrine when the Mahāsaṃghika school, which took shape at the time of the radical split, evolved into the Mahāyāna movement around the beginning of the Common Era, and the idea of the *tathāgata-garbha* or Buddha-nature, the high-water mark of Indian Mahāyāna, was developed through the *prajñā* scriptures. This is how I read Buddhist history.

Like the people of his age, or so the scholars inform us, Śākyamuni was seeking liberation from the endless cycle of rebirth; and once he had reached *nirvāṇa* and an enlightened understanding of *pratītya-samutpāda*, he organized what he had experienced and expounded it in the form of the "Four Truths" of suffering, the cause of suffering, the overcoming of suffering, and the path that leads to the overcoming of suffering. By and large there is nothing wrong with this account. No doubt Śākyamuni did seek liberation from the wheel of *saṃsāra* and the eternal rest of *nirvāṇa*. But what is of critical importance is that in the course of his quest for *nirvāṇa*, he came to an unexpected awakening, or *bodhi*. Once enlightened, *nirvāṇa* and *bodhi* are the same, but it was while Śākyamuni was seeking *nirvāṇa* that he achieved *bodhi*. And what is this *bodhi*? It is the "wisdom" of *nirvāṇa*, the "awareness" of the "original self" (or Buddha-nature) — in short, "original purity of mind." This "enlightenment" is the very life blood of the Buddhist teaching.

The error of what is sometimes called "Hīnayāna Buddhism" is that it failed to keep this one Great Matter at the center. It was the Mahāyāna movement that retrieved this *truly* Buddhist idea from the "primitive scriptures" and developed the notions of *prajñā* and *śūnyatā* around it.

SHAKU JŌKŌ RŌSHI'S "SANKŌRYŌ"

The New Mahāyāna I am expounding is nothing more than a contemporary version of *prajñā* Buddhism. I find it in the *Sankōryō* of the Śākyamuni Association founded by the great Shaku Jōkō Rōshi, teacher of my former master Osaka Kōryū Rōkan. Institutionally, the Śākyamuni Association is a legal entity, but the *rōshi's* real intention was to establish a religion of the heart that he called the Prajñā Sect. Since the brief text of the *Sankōryō* belongs to the roots of the New Mahāyāna, it is worth citing here:

> *Mahāprajñāpāramitā* is the primary meaning of the Buddhist Way. Inscribe it in your heart of hearts!
>
> Precept, Meditation, Wisdom — these three are the key to attaining the Way. Devote yourself to their practice in your heart of hearts!
>
> The fourfold vow of the bodhisattva is our basic vow. Dedicate yourself to it in your heart of hearts!

For all the Chinese elements in Zen Buddhism, its main focus is still the imitation of Śākyamuni. By putting the attainment of *bodhi* above all else and accepting responsibility in one's life for "the totality of the Buddha Dharma," one binds oneself directly to the enlightenment of Śākyamuni.

Shaku Jōkō Rōshi was a twentieth-century religious reformer who understood the goal of the way of the Buddha to lie in reaching the Great Wisdom, that is, in the "actual realization of the original self" where the mind is in its "original purity." Seeing no need for absolutes like "God" or "Buddha," refusing to comment on the survival of a soul after death, and eliminating all mythical religious elements from his teaching (which therefore also relieved him of the obligation to engage in demythifying), Shaku Rōshi held up Zen Buddhism as a religion relevant to the contemporary world. This was what he had in mind with his Prajñā Sect for the heart.

Mahāyāna Buddhism was first introduced to the general public of Europe and America through the efforts of Suzuki Daisetz Sensei.

As a world-teacher, Daisetz's message to the West came down to this: Your 2,000 years of Western culture is a marvel to behold. Since modern times we in the East have received great gifts from you, and now it is our turn to return the favor. The essence of your Western culture is *vijñāna*, or discriminating knowledge. The soul of our Eastern religion is *prajñā*, or nondiscriminating wisdom. As the progress of science makes it plain to see, *vijñāna* plays an important role for all of humanity. But without the guidance of *prajñā*, this knowledge turns around to destroy the humanity it is supposed to serve. Your culture has more than its share of *vijñāna*, but it is wanting in *prajñā*. And now we from the East will teach you about it.

Reflective people in the West turned an attentive ear to what Daisetz had to say, and as a result Zen has earned a place in the intellectual history of the world. But Daisetz's message went further than simply teaching the West about Eastern wisdom: It is not that there is no *prajñā* in the West. We find it, for example, in the sermons of Meister Eckhart. But this is exceptional and restricted to persons of special genius. What is absent is a way to guide ordinary men and women to attain it. The Buddha Dharma offers just such a way.

This is how I understand Shaku Jōkō Rōshi's three principles of Precept, Meditation, and Wisdom, which are really an abbreviation of the teaching of the Noble Eightfold Path that belongs to "early Buddhism." The vow to keep the precepts (*śīla*) has to do with regulating one's life. It attunes the totality of body-and-mind for entry into *zazen* or Zen meditation.[4] *Zazen* is neither a merely *psychological* unity nor is it a form of *contemplation*. It is a serene unity of body-mind out of which the wisdom of *prajñā* appears. One may thus

[4] For years now, Akizuki has criticized the use of the English term *meditation* because he feels it is always a transitive verb entailing an object, whereas Zen does not primarily think of itself as thinking *about* anything. See his *Under the Standard of the New Mahāyāna*, 154 (see above 5, n. 15). Having been assured by the translators that this is not necessarily the case in the Western religious tradition, he has given his consent to the use of this term.

speak of an "ascending path" of Precept→Meditation→Wisdom, although this way of speaking does not fully take into account the centrality of the Buddha Dharma.

In fact, all three principles issue out of appropriated wisdom or *prajñā*. It is the very self-initiating, self-unfolding of wisdom in *satori* that constitutes the true practice of the Buddha way.[5] This is the "descending path" of Wisdom→Meditation→Precept. A clear exposition of this process can be found in Zen Master Dōgen's idea of "the wondrous practice of original enlightenment."[6] Our Zen Master Hakuin prefers to put the primary stress on the practice of the "ascending path," although he opens his *Hymn to Zazen* with the words, "All sentient beings are originally Buddha," and later in the same piece speaks of "Opening the gates to where cause and effect are one."[7] In this sense he assumes the same standpoint of the "original purity" of the *satori* of Śākyamuni as Dōgen had.[8]

Dōgen says, "I, as original Buddha," practice the rule; it is not a matter of "*Thou shalt not do* evil," but of "*I do not do* evil." This is what Dōgen calls a manifestation of "the power not-to-do."[9] Here we see "keeping the *śīla*" as a self-initiating, self-unfolding of *prajñā*. In other words, *prajñā* is the *pāramitā* or perfection of following the precepts. Since it is the "I as Buddha" of original enlightenment who

---

[5] The description of wisdom as "self-initiating, self-unfolding" is taken directly from Nishida Kitarō's description of pure experience. See his *An Inquiry into the Good*, trans. by M. Abe and C. Ives (New Haven: Yale University Press, 1990).

[6] The phrase *wondrous practice of original enlightenment* (本証の妙修) is central to Dōgen's thought. Akizuki is here combining two terms found in the "Discourse on Practice" 弁道話) chapter of the *Shōbōgenzō*.

[7] "Cause" refers to sentient beings, "effect" refers to the Buddha or buddhahood. For a translation of the entire hymn, see Heinrich Dumoulin, *Zen Buddhism: A History*, vol. 2, *Japan* (New York: Macmillan, 1990), 393-94.

[8] On Dōgen, see my 道元入門 *[Introduction to Dōgen]*, and on Hakuin, my 白隠禅師 *[Zen Master Hakuin]*, both published by Kōdansha of Tokyo (1970, 1985).

[9] This appears in the 正法眼蔵随聞記 2.4. An English translation prepared by R. Masunaga was published under the title *A Primer of Soto Zen* (Honolulu, 1971).

do *zazen*, it cannot really be described as the act of sentient beings exerting supreme psychological effort to force themselves to sit, but as a "wondrous practice" of original enlightenment, a Zen meditation that has *Buddha as its subject.* This is the *"pāramitā* of meditation."

Zazen is not, therefore, a technique aimed at *satori* but, as Dōgen says, is *just sitting.*[10] It is a "*zazen* of the Buddha" where "body-mind is cast off." But "just sitting" is not just *sitting.* For Dōgen it means "noble activities are the Buddha Dharma at work, the working of the Dharma is religious practice."[11] Everyday life — or what the Chinese called *li* (ritual) — must itself be Buddha Dharma. It is "life-in-Zen," where "the everyday mind is the way."

This brings us to the final Great Matter. By practicing the three principles progressively as Precept→Meditation→Wisdom, one arrives at *bodhi.* And the "wisdom" of this *bodhi* functions in turn as Wisdom→Meditation, Wisdom→Precept. What then is the real meaning of the *satori* we call *prajñā?* It is a self-awareness of a self that is "originally pure." And what sort of self is it that can be referred to in its "original" sense?

In the end, everything boils down to the question, What is *satori?* When it is put to me this way, my answer is equally blunt, not the reply of a scholar but of one who practices Zen: *Satori* is the self-awareness of the original self, a self for which when there is no ego all is self. This is the raw fact of Zen experience — "original purity, original emptiness." As my principal master Yamada Mumon Rōshi said, when Śākyamuni looked at the morning star, he must have exclaimed, "Ah, I am twinkling." From the depths of meditation, in the

---

[10] See the "General Teachings for the Promotion of Zen" (普勧坐禅儀), where the well-known idea of "just sitting" (只管打坐) is spelled out. Regarding the idea of not-doing, see also the "Discourse on Practice" chapter of the *Shōbōgenzō* (30, n. 6 above) and the diary Dōgen kept in China (宝慶記). A richly annotated edition of the latter has been prepared by Takashi James Kodera, *Dōgen's Formative Years in China* (Boulder: Great Eastern Book Co., 1980).

[11] The reference here is to the opening lines of the "Noble Activities of Practicing Buddhas" (行仏威儀) chapter of the *Shōbōgenzō.*

realm of *anātman* and emptied of ego, the twinkling of the morning star catches the eye of Śākyamuni and *nothingness* breaks through into a kind of immediate intuition. This is the self-awareness of the "original self" in which "things and ego are one."

Śūnyatā, or emptiness, means that "self and other are not two." In *śūnyatā* I and Thou are distinct but inseparable. Because the pain of the other becomes the pain of the self, the enlightened one cannot stay put. Instead of abiding in *nirvāṇa* as a Hīnayāna *arhat*, the Mahāyāna bodhisattva must take the path of working for the salvation of all sentient beings. Of its nature, *prajñā* must overflow into compassion. Original enlightenment must become wondrous practice. This self-initiating, self-unfolding of *prajñā* is what makes it *pāramitā*.

We see this reflected in the fourfold vow of the bodhisattva, which I reproduce here:

> However innumerable sentient beings,
>   I vow to save them all.
> However inexhaustible the passions,
>   I vow to extinguish them all.
> However limitless the dharmas,
>   I vow to study them all.
> However infinite the Buddha Way,
>   I vow to attain it.

A SKETCH OF THE NEW MAHĀYĀNA

The "*prajñā* Buddha Dharma" we have been speaking of lies behind the words of Japan's ancient religious teacher, Prince Shōtoku: "This world is vain and fleeting, only Buddha is truth." Understanding these words is the first step on the road to a New Mahāyāna.

Because Buddhism begins from an insight into the transience of all the things of life, it naturally leads to the way of homelessness or taking leave of the world. Once it has been illuminated by the truth of the Buddha Dharma, the world shows itself to be false and transitory. The Buddha Dharma of the future — that is, for the New Mahāyāna — must be a *lay Buddhism*. But simple laicization alone will not do. Unless it also maintains the homelessness of the heart, it will die. The point is so important that it must be felt in the very fiber of one's being if we are to advocate a New Mahāyāna.

When Mahāyāna Buddhism was born around the beginning of the Common Era in India, it was as a reform movement centered on the laity and aided by a small number of homeless monks coming from the Mahāsaṃghika tradition, of which we spoke above. Wherever it spread, it put less stress on the minority of homeless monks than on the salvation of the greater masses of people. By nature, the Mahāyāna tradition was a "lay" Buddhism for those "at home." But with the passage of time, and before anyone realized what was happening, the monks emerged as a kind of professional class, homeless in name, lay in fact. This is the situation we find ourselves in today.

Just as any religious group needs its specialists, so too Mahāyāna Buddhism needs its lay-homeless monks. But since Buddhism is in essence a "religion of awakening," it poses necessary limits to the role of the professional teacher. When all is said and done, Buddhism is a matter of practicing *oneself*. It is always and forever a question of the awareness of one's *self*, which no teacher or specialist can ever replace. Muddleheaded spirits who complain, "But I am a sinful fool and have to rely on the words of holy people," will forever find the Buddha's way closed to them. Ultimately, there are no sinners or saints, only "original Buddha." To awaken to this fact in oneself is what Buddhism is all about. If you picked up this book in the hopes of learning something about the Buddha Dharma, it was not the sinful fool in you at work but the original Buddha. Stop and think about this for a moment. Switch channels in your mind and cease thinking about yourself as a poor mortal. It is the original Buddha who is reading — or reciting the phrase *Namu-amida-butsu* or *Namu-myōhō-rengekyō* or *Namu-Henshō-kongō* or *Mahāprajñāpāramitā*.

Formerly I spoke of the Buddha Dharma of the New Mahāyanā as "simply taking the posture of *zazen* and chanting *Mahāprajñāpāramitā*." In this book, as we shall see by and by, I am advocating the cultivation of a New Mahāyāna that begins from the *prajñā* Dharma

of Prince Shōtoku and includes the teachings of the three teachers
of New Kamakura Buddhism: Shinran, Nichiren, and Dōgen.[12]

Shinran's doctrine of "faith alone" — that one need only believe in
the original vow of Amida Buddha and invoke the six sacred syllables *Namu-amida-butsu* in order to be saved — delves deeply into the
interiority of human existence to find the *Prajñā* Dharma. It is a
teaching that can be held up proudly to other world religions.

Nichiren, a forerunner no less worthy of esteem than Shinran,
taught that the salvation of *Prajñā* Buddha Dharma consisted
merely in chanting the words *Namu-myōhō-rengekyō*. One of the
things we have to learn from Nichiren today is the importance he
gave to the *community* in contrast to Shinran's stress on the *individual*. Indeed, the communal element is critical for the Buddha
Dharma of the future. In imitation of Christianity, the Buddhism of
the New Mahāyāna must, as Hisamatsu Sensei has said, demon-
strate its power "to create history within history and beyond history"
for the sake of what Hakuin called "the erection of a Buddha land."

Finally, at the point where Shinran's interiority and Nichiren's ex-
teriority converge, I see the true core of Dōgen's *prajñā* Buddha.
This is why these three masters are to be studied after Prince Shōtoku.

A great deal remains to be said about the actual working of the lay
Buddhism of the New Mahāyāna, about its assault on the living "history" of religion, and about the matter of a religion of "humanity." It
is to these questions that we turn in the following chapters.

---

[12] See my little book, 在家禅のすすめ *[In Praise of Lay Zen]* (Tokyo: Kōsaidō,
1980)

3 Five Articles for a New Mahāyāna

If I remember correctly, the first time I used the term "New Mahā-yāna" in public was about ten years ago, when it appeared in the table of contents of a book I was writing called *In the Beginning Was the Great Compassion.*[1] But it was only after I had completed my *Collected Writings* that I took it up properly, in a little book called *In Praise of Lay Zen.*[2] The idea itself, as I have made clear in the previous chapter, is not my own but a distillation of the ideas of others who have gone before me on the path. I have taken it upon myself to call for a New Mahāyāna movement only because I am convinced it is a matter of grave urgency for Buddhism today.

In any case, a few years later, in 1986, I completed the 65th year of my life. As the saying goes, "The Zen monk does not come of age until 70." That meant I still had five years to go. I decided to take the occasion to devote my life from then on to the movement for a New Mahāyāna.

To give a quick sketch of what this has come to mean for me, I would like to reproduce here the "Proclamation-Prayer" that I have hanging on the wall of my place of retreat, Sokuhi-an. I will then comment at some length on each of the five articles that make it up.

[1] Vol. 2 of Akizuki's *Collected Writings*. See above, 19, n. 7.
[2] See above, 34, n. 12.

Five Vows for the Proclamation of a "New Mahāyāna"

To correct the mistaken notion of a "Buddhaless Mahāyāna"
and penetrate to the true spirit of Mahāyāna.

To relativize the absolutism of one's own religious sect and
return to the founder, Śākyamuni.

To enter into dialogue with other religions and cultivate the
ideal of a religion of humanity.

To take one's place self-consciously in a post-modern world
and erect a historical Buddha land.

To revere the true way of homelessness and bring about a
new lay Buddhist way.

In what remains of this chapter, I should like to spell out in more
concrete terms what these five articles of my prayer for a New Mahāyāna mean. Many of the details will have to wait for later chapters; here I will try to give as clear and straightforward an outline as
I can of what I see as the main thrust, and in that way to provide a
perspective to what follows.

TO CORRECT THE MISTAKEN NOTION OF A "BUDDHALESS MAHĀYĀNA" AND PENETRATE TO THE TRUE SPIRIT OF MAHĀYĀNA

Talk of a Buddhaless Mahāyāna has been around for some time now.
The idea is that since the Mahāyāna tradition only began several
centuries after the death of Śākyamuni the Buddha, the teachings
laid out in the Mahāyāna sūtras do not represent the *ipsissima verba*
of the historical Śākyamuni. This much no one disputes. From a literary and historical point of view, it is self-evident.

The problem is that many who hold this position today do not
stop there, but go on to swallow whole the modernist errors of European Buddhist studies. Let us return to the example I touched on in
the preceding chapter, citing the scholar's own words:

> Buddhism came twice to Japan. The first time was by way
> of Korea when it was transmitted through the Chinese Bud-
> dhist canon. This process began during the ancient times of

Emperor Kinmei and was carried into the early years of the Tokugawa period through the illustrious figure of Ingen Ryūki. The second time was when it entered Japan by way of modern Europe, transmitted through the Pāli Canon in ancient Indian languages. This latter transmission has enabled us for the first time to hear the true words of Śākyamuni.[3]

In other words, in addition to the first culture shock our ancient forbears experienced at coming into contact with the great Buddhist religion through China and Korea, we were put through a second culture shock in the Meiji era when we had our first contact through European scholarship with the Buddhist scriptures in their original language. This latter shock, whose after-effects are with us still, was twofold. On the one hand, those who knew only the Chinese canon were suddenly faced with the existence of the Buddhist canon in an ancient Indian language. On the other, they had to learn it not from Asia but through the academic world of Europe.

From the viewpoint of contemporary scholarship, the idea that in the Meiji period we Japanese were able for the first time to hear Śākyamuni speaking in his own words is so much hogwash. Indeed, scholars in Europe have argued vigorously that certain Chinese texts are older than the Pāli texts and more faithful to early Buddhism. What is more, the scholarship of modern Europe in general—and not only Buddhist scholarship—has come up for serious reexamination in a veritable swell of criticism.

Far from being "Buddhaless," Mahāyāna Buddhism transmits the true meaning of the *satori* of Śākyamuni in a much more impressive manner than so-called primitive Buddhism or the Hīnayāna brand of sectarian Buddhism. My idea is to call for clear thinking on the erroneous idea of a Buddhaless Mahāyāna in order to draw nearer to the spirit of "true Mahāyāna." And let there be no mistake about it, I consider the New Mahāyāna to be the *true* Mahāyāna. Religious *ref-*

---

[3] See Masutani Fumio 増谷文雄 , 仏教概論 [*An Outline of Buddhism*] (Tokyo: Chikuma Shobō, 1967). Ingen Ryūki 隠元隆琦 (Chin., Yin-yüan Lung-ch'i, 1592-1673) arrived in Japan at the advanced age of sixty-two.

ormations always take the form of a *restoration*. History and literature are respectable disciplines in their own right, but they do not suffice to generate an approach to Buddhist studies that comprehends the true meaning of Śākyamuni.

Here, as elsewhere, I avoid the term *primitive Buddhism* and prefer to speak of *early Buddhism*. The term *primitive Buddhism* is really little more than a neat and clever rearrangement of certain "true teachings of the historical Śākyamuni," skillfully crafted in the heads of high-minded university professors to gain respectability in modern European academia. This being so, I would go further to argue that we need to recover belief in the "seal of the Buddhist mind" that has been transmitted down through the patriarchs "from heart to heart." As Dōgen says, "to one who is enlightened, everyone is Śākyamuni." In the same sense, I would like to see Buddhist studies as the academic pursuit of *oneself as Śākyamuni*.

TO RELATIVIZE THE ABSOLUTISM OF ONE'S OWN RELIGIOUS SECT AND RETURN TO THE FOUNDER, ŚĀKYAMUNI

Up until now, Buddhism in Japan has been almost entirely a Buddhism of sectarian founders. The original founder, Śākyamuni, has been set up on a pedestal somewhere above the doctrines of the founders of the various sects that have developed in Japan from the time of the Heian and Kamakura periods. Within certain limits, this is acceptable. But when it erodes into "sectarian absolutism," everyone loses. As the proverbial saying goes, "No matter which religion wins, Śākyamuni is shamed."

In line with Dōgen's idea that "for the enlightened, everyone is Śākyamuni," the various sectarian founders inaugurated new religious movements. In this way, one and the same Buddha Dharma of Śākyamuni provided a common ground. To find one's way back to that common ground requires that one first *relativize* sectarian absolutism. The New Mahāyāna sees this task as a priority for Buddhism today.

More than a decade ago, the Catholic Church pulled back from its traditional stance of "universal Catholicism" in order to work for reunification with fellow Christians in the Protestant and Orthodox traditions. Concerted efforts have also been made towards dialogue with other religions. We are living in an age that urges us to follow such a "human course." But unless particular religious sects find a way to relativize their own tradition vis-à-vis the others, no dialogue in a true ecumenical spirit is possible—neither among religions nor within a particular religion.

When I here speak of relativizing sectarian absolutism so as to return to the founder Śākyamuni, I do not have in mind the "historical Śākyamuni" that the scholars of "primitive Buddhism" talk about. Some years ago Yamada Mumon Rōshi published a book entitled *Return to Śākyamuni*,[4] in which he advanced the idea that, once awakened to the "Buddha of the true tradition," one becomes oneself Śākyamuni ("for the enlightened, everyone is Śākyamuni"). In so doing, he was roundly criticized by these scholars for setting up an arbitrary Śākyamuni without taking into account the findings of history and literature. To be sure, anyone who sets out to paint a portrait of the Śākyamuni of history would be ill-advised to overlook the contributions of historical and literary research. All I wish to insist on is that Mumon Rōshi's "return to the Buddha" represents a valid approach in its own right.

However one may define Buddhist studies, I believe that it must include the tradition of the "triple learning"—Precept, Meditation, and Wisdom—or what Professor Tamaki Kōshirō has spoken of as a "rationality of the total person." As important as the scholarly deliverances of history and literature are for Buddhist studies, they remain subsidiary to the main matter: the absolute subjectivity of the enlightenment (*prajñā*) of the true individual (Buddha) through the triple learning. This is the reason for expanding the notion of rationality to include the disciplines of Precept and Meditation.

At the conclusion of the preceding chapter, I outlined a view of

---

[4] 釈尊にかえれ (Tokyo: Shunjūsha, 1967).

Japanese Buddhism combining key insights of Prince Shōtoku, Dōgen, Shinran, and Nichiren. To that I would only add that the pivot on which everything turns is the idea of a new *partnership,* a renewed sense of the interpersonal in matters of religion. This is what I take to be the next most important step in the historical development of Buddhism.[5]

TO ENTER INTO DIALOGUE WITH OTHER RELIGIONS AND CULTIVATE THE IDEAL OF A RELIGION OF HUMANITY

I have often spoken favorably of the new direction the Catholic Church has taken since the Second Vatican Council in recognizing the critical importance of dialogue with other religions and the irreplaceable role it can play in securing world peace. Of course, if Catholicism is held to be the only true way for the whole of the human race, things are much simpler. All one need do is herald the message, "Repent and make yourselves Catholic!" But this effectively slams the door in the face of dialogue and can only end in the sorry repetition of what has to count among the great stupidities of human history: wars of religion.

In terms of the distinction that scholars of religion draw between ethnic religions and world religions, Japanese Shinto belongs among the former. The late Japanese Empire that undertook the aggressive invasion of its neighbors under the noble banner of the "East Asian Co-Prosperity Sphere" set up Shinto shrines in Korea, Taiwan, and Singapore to promote Shinto throughout the region. The religion they were spreading was so thoroughly ethnic, however, that it was completely swallowed up in the final tragedies of the war. As a matter of fact, I believe that there is a great deal in Shinto—I exclude State Shinto here—that justifies classing it as a world religion, but that is somewhat far afield of our concerns here.

Entering into dialogue with other religions and holding up the

[5] See my これからの仏教 *[Buddhism from Here On]* (Osaka: Tōhō Shuppan, 1987).

ideal of a religion of humanity does not mean setting up one great religion for the whole of the human race. It aims only at promoting a forum for dialogue among like-minded world religions in the present world in order to uncover what there is of "common ground" among them. This is all I mean by the term *religion of humanity*.

The celebrated English scholar Arnold Toynbee, reputed to be the greatest historian of our century, had the following to say at the conclusion of a famous speech:

> When historians a thousand years hence look back on the twentieth century and ask what was most distinctive about it, they will not remember it for the great face-off between liberalism and communism but as the century in which the encounter between Buddhism and Christianity began.[6]

It was Toynbee's fervent hope that the dialogue between Buddhism and Christianity, between East and West, that began in the twentieth century would lead people to the discovery of a deeper, common humanity that would be remembered into the next millennium.

In fact, the dialogue between Christianity and Buddhism is being conducted on a global scale today. A couple of years ago, Professor David Chappell from the University of Hawaii came to Japan to assist in preparations for a triennial international conference on Buddhism and Christianity. On that occasion he remarked apropos of the change in climate: "A decade ago there were only 30 or 40 universities in the United States offering courses on Buddhism, but now there are hundreds of them. And even those who are doing doctoral studies in Christian theology are commonly obliged to study Buddhist doctrine."

Undoubtedly Buddhism and Christianity share a vast expanse of common ground. The "Christ in me" of which Paul speaks when he writes, "It is not I that live but Christ who lives in me" (Gal. 2:20),

---

[6] Despite the best efforts of the author and translators, this famous quote, popularly attributed to Toynbee, could not be located in the original, though we did find variant versions. *Si non è vero, è ben trovato.*

may be considered as referring to the very same religious reality as "the true person of no rank" of whom Lin-chi speaks. For Paul, "Christ in me" represents the true subject of the self, the "original self" that belongs to the common ground between Buddhism and Christianity.[7] (Otherwise I can only think of his "possession" by Christ as of a kind with popular belief in possession by animals.)

The discovery of common ground between two religions does not justify rushing to the conclusion that the two are saying exactly the same thing. When a Catholic priest practices *zazen*, for example, and claims to have accomplished the Great Matter, this does not justify the conclusion that the same person is at one and the same time a Catholic priest and a proper Rinzai Zen master. I have serious doubts about the consistency of such a posture. Similarly, there are those who draw on the medieval Christian mystics in the attempt to fuse the notions of "God" and "Absolute Nothingness."[8] But is not Meister Eckhart still held to be a heretic by the Catholic Church, despite all the talk about lifting the condemnation against him? If we are to seek common ground between Buddhism and Christianity, therefore, it would be folly not to remain alert to their inflexible differences as well.

TO TAKE ONE'S PLACE SELF-CONSCIOUSLY IN A POST-MODERN WORLD AND ERECT A HISTORICAL BUDDHA LAND

This fourth article echoes the "post-modern" standpoint proclaimed by Hisamatsu Shin'ichi Sensei and follows the line of his FAS Zen. Around the end of the middle ages and the beginning of the modern age, people had the sense that one era had ended and a new period in history was upon them. So, too, it is becoming apparent to more

---

[7] This comparison with St. Paul has been a favorite one among the Kyoto philosophers since the time of Nishida Kitarō.

[8] The reference is to a subject much discussed in connection with the Kyoto school and a book by the same name published out of these discussions by the Nanzan Institute for Religion and Culture, 絶対無と神 (Tokyo: Shunjūsha, 1981).

and more of us that humanity has arrived at the end of the modern age and is standing on the threshold of a post-modern world.

One of the great philosophers of the twentieth century, Karl Jaspers, spoke of "humanity breaking into the second axial age." The first axial age saw the rise of the agricultural revolution and the appearance of the city states. In the absence of a spiritual civilization to respond to the needs of that age, there arose as teachers of humanity Socrates, Confucius, and Buddha. (Jaspers includes the second Isaiah in their ranks as a forerunner of Jesus.) And now we find ourselves about to enter into a second axial age with all the splendors of material culture made possible by the industrial revolution. Here too, in the absence of an adequate spiritual civilization to accompany this change, new teachers of humanity are being called for. As before, Western culture alone cannot answer this need. The world is placing great hope in the wisdom of the East — in the *prajñā* that D. T. Suzuki opposed to *vijñāna*.

The four world sages of the first axial period answered the need for a spiritual revolution to accompany the material advance of the agricultural revolution. In our own day a new Buddha and new Christ are desperately needed to effect a spiritual revolution to heal the crippling material progress of industrialization. Jaspers felt himself deep down to be a "prophet to make straight the way of the lord." Who will be the new teacher of the post-modern world? I repeat: we cannot look only to the West for an answer. A new lord of humanity is also being sought from within the wisdom of the East.

A Buddhist response to this situation must include not only the *individual* dimension stressed by Shinran but also the *communal* dimension stressed by Nichiren. This is what our Rinzai Master Hakuin meant by the phrase, "The noble deeds of the bodhisattva are the source of the Buddha land."[9] Or again, Hisamatsu Sensei's post-modern concerns naturally led him to a standpoint that would embrace all of humanity, the standpoint of what he called "the absolute subject, constructor of the historical Buddha land." My point is that

---

[9] This phrase is used frequently in Hakuin's *Vernacular Sermons* 仮名法語 .

religion today can no longer afford to concern itself exclusively with the heart and soul of the individual. Indeed, it was for that very reason that Mahāyāna Buddhism came to be known as the "Great Vehicle."

What I refer to in my second article as the return to Śākyamuni corresponds to Hisamatsu Sensei's "awareness of the formless self" (what we have been calling above "original self"). The ideal of a religion of humanity mentioned in my third article corresponds to his "standpoint of all of humanity." And the erection of a historical Buddha land in my fourth article is nothing other than Hisamatsu Sensei's "creating history by transcending history." It was only later that I noticed the parallel between my Five Articles for a New Mahāyāna and Hisamatsu Sensei's FAS (Formless Self—All Humanity—Superhistorical History).

My prayer for a New Mahāyāna shares in Hisamatsu Sensei's vision as a post-modernist: to modernize what needs to be modernized and to overcome the "sickness unto death" of the idea of the "ego" that lurks at the bottom of European modernity. It is a vision for a historical Buddha land different from any that has existed in religion up to the present, a Buddha land fully alive *in the reality of history*, neither an *other-worldly* spiritual Buddha land nor a *this-worldly* intellectual Buddha land of *this world*.

TO REVERE THE TRUE WAY OF HOMELESSNESS AND BRING ABOUT A NEW LAY BUDDHIST WAY

The New Testament speaks of persons who have chosen to remain celibate "for the sake of the Kingdom of God."[10] I have the greatest respect for those pure monks who have managed to keep the *vinaya*, the rule of life established by Śākyamuni for life in the *sangha*. Given

---

[10] See Matthew 19:11-12. "Not all men can receive this precept, but only those to whom it is given. For there are eunuchs who have been so from birth, and there are eunuchs who have been made eunuchs by men, and there are eunuchs who have made themselves eunuchs for the sake of the kingdom of heaven. He who is able to receive this, let him receive it."

all the deception that goes on, I can only stand in awe of pure monks who abide by the rule strictly. Masters who oblige young monks to keep a monastic rule while they themselves keep a secret wife, smoke, drink, and eat red meat on the sly, set an appalling example. Those that do not marry are hardly much better. For the *vinaya,* an affair is an affair, self-abuse is self-abuse. Zen monks of today, as of old, have been masters at cheating. There is the time-worn practice, for example, of "woman begging," a rather crude euphemism for taking care of one's sexual appetites. This kind of making light of homelessness has a long way to go to reach the "love and purity" of the Japanese Protestant tradition. If one has to cheat, then take a wife and do it openly! At the same time, for the pure monk, who does not take a wife in the flesh, deliberately to look down on "the profane of the world," even in the slightest, is a compromise of his purity. Verily, "Buddha means not-knowing."

The vow to practice the *vinaya* as a temple monk is basic for the Hīnayāna *bhikku.* Even today the monks of the Southern Theravāda tradition follow this style of life. In contrast to the *bhikku* arhat, Mahāyāna takes as its central vow the salvation of all sentient beings, revering the way of the bodhisattva, "obscuring the light and mixing with the dust, ashes on the head and face to the ground."[11] Thus true Mahāyāna Buddhism finds more meaning in the way of life of the laity at large than in the life led by some pure *bhikku* or other.

Mahāyāna Buddhism is by nature a lay Buddhism which requires a homelessness of the heart to hold the terms *lay* and *Buddhist* together. Without this homelessness of the heart, the words of Prince Shōtoku about the vain and fleeting falsity of the world would be pointless. Without it Buddhism would cease to be Buddhist, because the basic principle that "only Buddha is truth" would have been forsaken. The way of homelessness is all-important to Buddhism — if not in a physical sense, then at least in a spiritual one.

As for the matter of the "rule," I myself have renounced the

---

[11] A phrase quoted often in Mahāyāna Buddhism but found originally in the works of Lao-tzu.

bhikku vinaya and teach that the "Mahāyāna bodhisattva rule" suffices to become a monk in the tradition of "Mahāyāna rule alone." That is to say, I am advocating a new lay Mahāyāna way that lives within the world of "fleeting vanity" as the "one Buddha" that "is truth." Though it is called a "lay" Buddhism, it does not distinguish between monks and laity. If specialists are somehow called for, then it is all right to designate them occupationally as monks, even though, to borrow the words of Shinran, they are "neither monk nor laity." In order to bring about this nondiscriminating form of lay Mahāyāna, we need to rediscover the Japanese Tendai tradition of accepting the "Mahāyāna rule alone."[12]

I am not alone in this way of thinking about the *vinaya*. Dōgen also chose this way, rationally and fully aware of what he was doing. Consistently refusing to acknowledge the traditional Nara rule that had been transmitted by Ganjin, a master in the Chinese Nan-shan (southern mountain) *vinaya* school,[13] Dōgen relied on the "Mahāyāna rule alone" of Mount Hiei's Saichō, even though he himself followed the life of a pure monk in strict observance of the Hīnayāna *vinaya* by keeping the precepts for his entire life. The same applies to the rigorous life of practice led by the religious reformer and saintly monk of the Shōwa era, Shaku Jōkō. For my part, I am prepared to take the next step and renounce the Hīnayāna *vinaya* in order to advocate the "Mahāyāna rule alone."

In the foregoing I have tried to lay out in extremely simple form the five articles of my prayer for a New Mahāyāna. Each article harbors large and difficult questions, which in due time will have to be spelled out if they are to elicit the general criticism they need.

---

[12] Saichō 最澄 (767-822), the transmitter of the T'ien-t'ai school and founder of Japanese Tendai, rejected the *vinaya* practices of the Nara temples and taught the sufficiency of the Mahāyāna bodhisattva precepts alone.

[13] Ganjin 鑑真 (688-763) is credited with officially transmitting the precepts to Japan in the 8th century.

The Return to Śākyamuni

4   Who is Śākyamuni?

THE ERROR OF MODERN BUDDHISM

In the foregoing chapters, I proposed as the first element of a New
Mahāyāna the need to correct the idea of a Buddhaless Mahāyāna
by presenting Mahāyāna as the Buddha Dharma that has carried on
the true meaning of the preaching of Śākyamuni; and as a second element, the need to correct the error of Japanese Buddhism's sectarian absolutism by recognizing the relativity of particular sects and
returning to the original founder, Śākyamuni. Now I would like to
turn to this latter theme by having a look at what the Buddha said,
or at least what I understand the Dharma (the truth or teaching) of
the Buddha to be. Compared with the material presented in the
foregoing chapters, the problem of the return to Śākyamuni and my
view of his Dharma may be less familiar and require something more
in the way of introduction.

The problem is actually twofold. On the one hand, it has to do
with the *source materials* by which we know about Śākyamuni; and
on the other, with the *subjective position* from which we review these
materials.

It would appear that the only source materials at our disposal that
give us a glimpse of the Śākyamuni of history are the five-part
Nikāya, which belongs among the *Āgama* sūtras transmitted in Pāli
by the Southern Theravāda tradition, and the four-part Chinese
translation of the same set of scriptures, the *Agon-kyō*. The argument that the five parts in Pāli alone present us with the actual ser-

mons of Śākyamuni is, as we have already noted, a dated one. There is no longer any doubt that the lopsided devotion of Southern Theravāda to the *Nikāya* is in error.

That having been said, the equally indisputable fact remains that historical materials for knowing about the Buddha depend exclusively on the *Āgama* sūtras, by which I mean to include both the Pāli *Nikāya* and their Chinese translations. The proper methodology for specialists in the field, it seems to me, is to make use of textual criticism to determine basic source materials, which historical and philological research can work on to yield the relatively most "ancient form of the transmission (*āgama*)." On that basis, it should be possible to get a new picture of the total historical development of Buddhism, and hence a better idea of the "fundamental Buddhist teachings" and a truer image of "early Buddhism."

Directing attention to the total historical development of Buddhism implies that Buddhism is not something that belongs to Śākyamuni alone (the fundamental Buddhist teachings), and that it is surely not to be restricted to what is contained in early Buddhism or the doctrine of the scriptural canon (what I just referred to as the relatively most ancient form of the transmission) compiled by the monastic communities of *bhikku* after Śākyamuni's death. In short, I am convinced that the total historical development of Buddhism ancient and new, north and south, east and west—both the overall panorama and the vital spirit that permeates it—represents real Buddhism in the true sense of the term. It is precisely as part of the quest for such a picture that the basic source materials of the *Āgama* have to be reexamined.

This is why, even though I am in provisional agreement with the theory that the *Āgama* represents the one and only source for our knowledge of the historical Śākyamuni, I am uneasy about the qualification "one and only."

When scholars of so-called primitive Buddhism read the *Nikāya* and extract from there what they call "primitive Buddhism," they do so through the rationalistic eyes of the modern European ego. Having been raised in environments where the Buddhist tradition is absent, they lack the "eye of enlightenment" — or what we call "the sūtra-reading inner eye"[1] — and therefore seek to explain Buddhism in terms of the rational categories of modern Europe. They, and the Japanese scholars that have trained under them, put on the glasses of the "modern ego" in order to read the *Nikāya*. To make matters worse, they do not realize what they are doing. I consider this a grave error, and indeed it is one of the reasons I find it necessary to consider Buddhism from a *post*-modern perspective.

In sum, I find two problems with the "primitive Buddhism" approach. First, it assumes that the *Nikāya* of the Southern Theravāda tradition represents the one and only source material, thus passing over the important Chinese translation of the *Agon* sūtras and hence failing to give the whole historical development of Buddhism its due. And second, lacking the proper sūtra-reading eye to study the literary sources, it arbitrarily constructs a "Śākyamuni of history" that in fact is simply an intellectual fabrication of the modern ego, tailored to the needs of professional academics.

WHERE IS ŚĀKYAMUNI TO BE FOUND?

Where do we turn then in our attempt to return to Śākyamuni? For if it is indeed the Śākyamuni of history that we seek, and if there is evidence at odds with the historical portrait painted for us by the scholars of primitive Buddhism, how do we go about looking for it? And how will we know when we have found it? Just who *is* this Śākyamuni?

Earlier I made passing reference to Dōgen's idea of a communication that can take place "only between a Buddha and a Buddha." The idea hearkens back to a passage in the *Lotus Sūtra* which reads:

> Only a Buddha can transmit to a Buddha
> and only a Buddha understands the truth entirely.[2]

---

[1] The term Akizuki uses here, 看経の眼 , appears frequently in the *Records of Lin-chi*. See also the "Sūtra Reading" (看経) chapter of the *Shōbōgenzō*.

[2] See above, 24, n. 2.

The point is that only a Buddha can know a Buddha; or in other words, that unless one become a Buddha, there is no way to know about the Buddha. As the saying goes:

> To know of the Buddha, ask the Buddha.
> To know of the chrysanthemum, ask the chrysanthemum.[3]

On this point, Dōgen says:

> The Buddha Dharma cannot be understood through rational and intellectual study. None who has looked at Buddhism in this way has ever attained enlightenment. Neither of the two vehicles can explain the Dharma, for it is the Buddha alone who can do so. The *Lotus Sūtra* says, "Only a Buddha can transmit to a Buddha, and only a Buddha understands the truth entirely."[4]

And elsewhere:

> "All Buddhas" refers to Śākyamuni Buddha. He symbolizes all the past, present, and future Buddhas. Śākyamuni is "The mind is directly Buddha."[5]

Dōgen is not alone in advancing this idea of "Śākyamuni the Buddha." The *Lotus Sūtra* makes a distinction between the "Śākyamuni as Traces" and the "Original Śākyamuni."[6] The former refers to the Śākyamuni of history, a man who lived in the fifth century BCE in

---

[3] From the "Seal of Transmission" (嗣書) chapter of the *Shōbōgenzō*.

[4] From the "Only between a Buddha and a Buddha" (唯仏与仏) chapter of the *Shōbōgenzō*.

[5] From the "The Mind is Directly Buddha" (即心是仏) chapter of the *Shōbōgenzō*.

[6] The *Lotus Sūtra* is traditionally understood as consisting of two parts: the first half on the "traces" of the Buddha, which expounds on the historical manifestations and teachings of Śākyamuni; and the second half on the "original" Buddha, which treats the "trans-historical" eternal Buddha. This is the origin of the phrase *honji-suijaku* 本地垂迹 , which describes the syncretistic Japanese religious idea that the Buddhas are underlying, transmundane realities, and the native deities of Japan are the historical "traces" or manifestations of the Buddhas.

India, left home at the age of twenty-nine, attained the Great Enlightenment at age thirty-five and became the Buddha, preached for
forty-five years, and passed away at eighty. The latter refers to what
is called "the Śākyamuni of enlightenment in the distant past,"[7] the
Śākyamuni of "original enlightenment" who became a Buddha in
the distant past and transcends the rhythms of time and history. According to Buddhist doctrine, the latter is called the *dharma-kāya*
("Dharma Body") of the Buddha and the former the *nirmāṇa-kāya*
("Correspondence Body"). The two are distinguishable but inseparable. They are also historically irreversible in the sense that the
dharma-kāya is prior and the *nirmāṇa-kāya* later. Thus the *formless*
Dharma Body took on the *visible* form of the Correspondence Body
and became manifest in this world in response to the need of sentient beings. This is what is normally meant by speaking of the
nirmāṇa-kāya (also called the Transformation Body) of the Buddha.
The final body that fills out the "three-body" doctrine (*trikāya*) is
the Reward Body (*sambhoga-kāya*). The Reward Body is generally
associated with Amida Buddha in contrast to the Correspondence
Body of Śākyamuni and the Dharma Body of the idealized, universal
figure of Mahāvairocana-tathāgata. In a certain sense Śākyamuni
may also be spoken of as the Reward Body inasmuch as it was as a reward for becoming a monk and practicing that he became the enlightened Buddha, which is his Reward Body.

Although this discussion has sidetracked us somewhat from our
main line of thought, my point was only to note that Dōgen's idea of
Śākyamuni Buddha and the three-body doctrine are explanations
for what Buddhism means by "Buddha" in the broad sense of the
term. For it is precisely on this basis that I wish to claim that to be a
scholar of Buddhism one must *become Śākyamuni*, so that "the mind
is directly Buddha."[8] In this sense, the *scholar* of *true* Buddhism must

---

[7] This phrase is used in the second half of the *Lotus Sūtra* to describe the trans-
historical reality of the Buddha.

[8] The words are a translation of one of the chapters of the *Shōbōgenzō*. See
above, 53, n. 5.

be "Buddha." It is quite as Dōgen says: "The Buddha Dharma is not something for people to know; the unenlightened cannot awaken to the Buddha Dharma."[9] The ignorant and sinful are not Buddha. By the same token, those who happen to be scholars, no matter how much they have to say about Buddhism, are not necessarily engaged in true *Buddhist* studies.

INTEGRATING TWO KINDS OF ZEN STUDIES

My friend the scholar Yanagida Seizan, when he was still professor of Zen studies at Hanazono University, is reported once to have remarked to the deceased president of Shunjūsha Publishing Company, Kanda Ryōichi, "There can be other kinds of Zen studies than what Akizuki calls Zen studies." Quite so, as I later told Mr. Kanda. At the time Yanagida had broken with his teacher, Hisamatsu Shin'ichi Sensei, to study Chinese Zen with the tools of history and literature. The scholarly studies he was churning out one after the other seemed closer in methodology to Tokyo University's Ui Hakuju Sensei than to the scholars of his neighboring Kyoto University. As things turned out, "Yanagida's Zen history" was to become world-renowned, far surpassing the influence of Dr. Ui.[10]

I am not one to reject the objectivistic methods of modern European historical and literary scholarship. But to turn Yanagida's words around, it is just *this* kind of Zen studies that I am inclined to

---

[9] Cited from the "Only between a Buddha and a Buddha" chapter of the *Shō-bōgenzō*.

[10] Ui Hakuju 宇井伯寿 was one of the pioneers of modern Buddhist studies in Japan (see below, 127-28). Akizuki has referred to Yanagida Seizan 柳田聖山 elsewhere as "the leading world authority on the historical study of Zen, particularly Chinese Zen" (*Zen Master Hakuin* [see above 30, n. 8], 104). Indeed, Yanagida's historical studies on Zen have revolutionized the modern understanding of the history and development of Zen Buddhism. One might mention, for example, his 初期禅宗史書の研究 [*Studies in the Historical Texts of Early Zen*] (Kyoto: Hōzōkan, 1967) and 臨済録 [*The record of Lin-chi*], 仏典講座 30 (Tokyo: Daizō Shuppansha, 1972). Yanagida is former director of Kyoto University's Institute for the Humanities.

characterize as Zen studies of "another kind." I once made the point forcefully that if one intends to do Zen studies as a follower of Rinzai Zen, one should first practice kōan Zen until one has completed the Great Matter (Hakuin's "system of kōan") and become a qualified Zen master.[11] It was against just this view that Yanagida's comment was directed.

Say, for instance, that one is writing about Bodhidharma. No matter how splendidly one lines up the historical and literary evidence to paint a picture of "the historical Bodhidharma" from the standpoint of modern Buddhist studies, we do not end up with the *living* reality of who Bodhidharma was. We have still to ask: Where is the true Bodhidharma? Who could he really have been?

A verse by Setchō Rōshi in the first case of the famous kōan collection known as the *Hekiganroku* ends with the words:

> The master looks around:
> "Is the patriarch there?
> —Yes! Bring him to me,
>   and he can wash my feet."[12]

This is how the disciple of Zen speaks about Bodhidharma. That is, if the mind has not become Buddha, then one is not talking about the Bodhidharma who actually lived. This is why it is said that "Śākyamuni and Bodhidharma are still practicing."

Now if that were all there is to be said about the matter, Śākyamuni and Bodhidharma would both end up as co-equals of the "Dharma body" between whom no distinction whatsoever remains. In fact, of course, Śākyamuni and Bodhidharma were individuals, each with his own distinctive character. Both need to be seen as real, *historical* individuals. The historical Śākyamuni and the Śākyamuni "enlightened in the distant past" must be "distinct but insepa-

---

[11] This means ascending to the rank of a patriarch and receiving qualification as a master.

[12] Cited in *Two Zen Classics (Mumonkan & Hekiganroku)*, trans. with commentaries by Katsuki Sekida (Tokyo: Weatherhill, 1977), 148.

rable." They can never be the same, but neither can they ever be apart.

Let us now have a look at the function of historical and literary "science" in its European, objectivist form. Around the time that Yanagida made the comment just cited, his criticism against the followers of Zen led him to the now famous turn of phrase: "It's like trying to drive a high-class imported automobile through a muddy field." No doubt this reflects the genuine sentiments of Yanagida at the time, filled as he was with a sense of mission for erecting a new, scientific approach to Zen studies. He had just broken ties with his honored teacher, Hisamatsu Shin'ichi Sensei, whom he had idolized from his youth — an event which occasioned some discord among the other principals in the Hisamatsu circle. Indeed, most scholars of his age-group engaged in Buddhist studies at the Universities of Kyoto and Tokyo had, like Yanagida, been attracted at first by genuine Buddhist scholars like Hisamatsu Sensei and entered academic pursuits with their minds set on following the Buddhist way. In no time at all, they found themselves drawn in the direction of more objective study. Examples of this shift are numerous, and I have no objection as far as it goes. My point is that it does not go far enough. As was to be expected, Yanagida returned to the bosom of his honored teacher in Hisamatsu Sensei's declining years and was on hand to record his "deathbed testimony."

To my way of thinking, *true* Zen studies entails a handshake between the idea of Akizuki and that of Yanagida. When I stop to think how, both for reflective scholars at home in Japan and abroad, the modern European idea of science is going through its *douleurs d'enfantement* in the "creation of a new science," I am myself convinced that Buddhist studies must also search self-consciously for a "new Buddhist studies."

The first focal point for such a renewal falls on *the subject doing the scholarship*. It brings into question just *who* it is that is carrying on Buddhist studies. I believe that it must be the "Buddha" (enlightened one) of whom it is said "only a Buddha communicates with a Buddha." The Śākyamuni who is meant in the injunction to "return to Śākyamuni" must be the Śākyamuni of the self in the here-and-now, the "mind that is directly Buddha."

To be sure, cars have an easier time on well-paved roads than they do in the mud. On the other hand, the asphalt paving kills whatever it is laid over. Is this really the only kind of road fit for people to walk on? Is it not high time we had a second look at what we are doing? History and literature need a renaissance. A new Buddhist studies has to be created.

In any event, it is my aim here to begin with the problem of the subject of scholarship and from there go on to consider, honestly and with an open mind, what strict scientific and literary researches have turned up in their study of the *Āgama*. Once that is done, the next step is to re-read the source materials with a new "sūtra-reading eye" and, focused on the whole historical development of Buddhism, to discover the true "law" of "Śākyamuni."

5 Causality and Karma

FROM THE RULE OF THE GODS TO THE AWARENESS OF KARMIC RETRIBUTION

Śākyamuni awakened to the truth, and became the first Buddha (enlightened one) in the history of humankind. After that, he went on to proclaim to others the Dharma that he had realized on his own. And so it was that 2,500 years ago Buddhism came to be established by Śākyamuni as a distinct religion.

As extraordinary a personality as this Śākyamuni was, he did not start from scratch. Nothing is ever totally unrelated to its historical circumstances, and the Buddha was no exception. There was a whole world of intellectual and philosophical history that had preceded him. The Indian notion of causality—the cause-and-effect workings of karmic retribution—is a key example of the legacy of ideas to which Śākyamuni fell heir.

The idea of karmic retribution had long been a part of Indian thought and as such was taken over as one of the basic assumptions of Buddhism. It is present in the Upaniṣads fully two or three centuries prior to the appearance of Buddhism. In the earlier period of the Brāhmaṇas, it was thought that people's fortunes and misfortunes were determined by the will of the gods. There is a common misconception among the Japanese that since India was the homeland of the Buddha, there must be no belief in gods in India. But like the ancient Japanese, who believed in a multitude of gods long before Buddhism found its way to them, the Indians, too, had a long tradition of polytheism. In fact, the will of the gods has played a greater role in Indian history through the centuries than the teachings of the Buddha have.

Buddhism, therefore, does not represent the mainstream of Indian thought. It may have touched the minds and hearts of the people of India religiously for over a thousand years, but it was always considered heretical. For Buddhism did not recognize the authority of the Vedas, the sacred texts of the Indo-Aryans, nor did it teach a faith in the supreme god Brahman and the other gods. What is more, Buddhism rejected the caste system which served as the basic structure of Indian society. According to its orthodox system of "Brahmanism," or "Hinduism," as it is currently known, the Buddha Śākyamuni is recognized as only one saint among many.

Be that as it may, throughout the period of the Upaniṣads two or three hundred years before the birth of the Buddha, the Indian people had a well-established theory of causality and karmic retribution. The fate visited on people was thought to be determined by the will of the gods, which in turn was influenced by the correct performance of rites. Not surprisingly, the Brahman class who performed these rites became the central social caste. Eventually the Kṣatriya (or royal, military caste) gained political power. This group came to a more acute awareness of the "self" and developed a more rational conception of the fate of humankind, which accounts for the theory of karma found in the Upaniṣads. According to this theory, the fate of humankind in general as well as of the individuals who make it up is not controlled by the will of the gods but is determined by the particular deeds of particular men and women. This idea of "causality" or "karmic retribution" teaches that good causes lead to good results and evil causes lead to evil results, or more accurately, that good deeds result in pleasure and evil deeds result in pain.

Ethically speaking, the belief that one's fate depends on the "will of the gods" is a form of heteronomy. In this regard it is not unlike heteronomous ethics of the Western middle ages. In the modern world, of course, we have come to think in terms of "free will" and the idea that each individual is responsible for his or her own fate.

This "awakening of the ego" is said to have given birth to the flowering of modern Western culture as we know it. When we turn to India, however, we find that such an awakening had already taken place two or three centuries prior to the birth of Buddhism. What is remarkable is not only that this development came about as early as it did, but also that it came about in confrontation with a belief in ethical heteronomy.

The autonomous theory of karmic retribution emphasized free will and brought with it a sense of the responsibility of individuals for their own actions. Such an approach was much more reasonable than the belief that one's fate was decided by the will of the gods and thus entirely out of one's own hands. At the same time, the theory presented a new problem. If one assumes karmic retribution, then one expects that good people will prosper and enjoy life, while the wicked will suffer and grow weak. But it is obvious that the exact opposite is quite often the case: the wicked flourish and get rich while the good suffer ignominiously. In the face of evidence to the contrary, how could anyone believe such a preposterous notion?

The answer lies in seeing karmic retribution as a causality that works itself out *through time*. Karma operates across the ages — past, present, and future — as individual beings are reborn and transmigrate through the six "destinies" of the realm of delusion: hell, hungry ghosts, beasts, *asura*, human beings, and divine beings.[1] The first three of these destines are called the "three evil paths," and together with the realm of the *asura* are known as the "four evil destinies." Beings in these four destinies experience only suffering and no pleasure. In contrast, the realm of divine beings (in Sanskrit, *deva*) consists of only pleasure and no suffering. The *asura* were originally a kind of divine being, but were degraded to a position below the gods

---

[1] It should be pointed out here, however, that these "gods" were not absolute deities like a Yahweh or Allah. Their temporary residence in the heavenly realm is a reward for good deeds in the past, but once their stock of good karma has been depleted, they will fall back into one of the evil destinies. Hence it was believed that even the gods could not escape from the suffering of the cycle of birth and death.

and human beings, and hence came to be referred to as the "non-heavenly." Finally, human beings, our realm of existence, belong to a destiny of great suffering but not without a certain amount of pleasure and joy.

"Causes and results follow one after the other like the turning of a wheel." Through the law of causality, sentient beings are caught as it were in a web of the karma spun by their own actions. Over and over they go through birth and death in the six destinies, enjoying the pleasant results of their good activities and suffering the retribution of their evil activities. This is known as *transmigration* or *metempsychosis*, the idea that sentient beings must suffer rebirths and deaths without end.

Even if one is reborn in the divine realm as a result of numerous good deeds and is able to enjoy a pleasurable existence during that one life, once the accumulated good karma has been exhausted, one is bound to fall back into one of the three evil destinies. Like the wizard of Kume,[2] who used up all his good karma the moment he caught a glimpse of the exposed thighs of a young maiden washing clothes at the river and, having lost the power to fly, fell to the earth, the gods too were believed to be so weak that even they were liable to get caught in the cycle of transmigration through the realms of delusion.

COMMON ELEMENTS IN THE NEW RELIGIONS OF BUDDHISM

The Buddhism of the establishment is dead. The monks either earn their living by performing funerals or other ceremonies for the dead, or feed off the treasures left them by their predecessors, extracting "entrance fees" from tourists visiting their temples and gardens. Meantime, the "New Religions" of Buddhism appear to be alive and

---

[2] This story is a familiar part of Japanese folklore, the earliest reference to it appearing in the *Fusō ryakki* 扶桑略記, an 11th-century history by the Hiei monk Kōen.

well. They teach the Dharma, build schools and hospitals, and take an active role in social movements.

A close examination of the beliefs and practices of the New Religions active today turns up three common elements: curses from the spirit world (*tatari*), patronage (*okage*), and healing.

We see the belief in *tatari* at work, for example, when a household is struck by some misfortune and a member of a New Religion quickly appears on the scene to blame the whole thing on the family's neglect of its ancestors. As we remarked back in chapter 1, the fear of such curses in Japan goes back to ancient times. The people of the early Heian period sought to pacify the vengeful spirit of Sugawara no Michizane[3] by enshrining him as a *kami*, Tenjin. Kanda Myōjin is a *kami* who was enshrined out of fear of the curse of Taira no Masakado.[4] These are just two examples of a longstanding "belief in vengeful spirits."

When questioned whether one's spirit survives after death, Śākyamuni refused to comment because he did not recognize the existence of gods that rule the fate of humankind and the world, nor did he speak of any "spirit" that survives death and transmigrates through other lives. *In this sense*, Śākyamuni was an atheist and rejected all belief in the world of spirits.

The idea that people fall into this misfortune or that because of a failure to venerate some ancestor or other is a consummate fiction that has nothing at all to do with Buddhist teaching. In comparison, the idea of causality or karmic retribution proposed by Indians 2,500 years ago, that one's fortune or misfortune is determined by one's karma, looks strikingly *modern* and rationalistic. It pains me to see how many Japanese are unable to extricate themselves from the

---

[3] Sugawara no Michizane 菅原道真 (845–903) was an accomplished scholar and figure of the Heian court who was forced into exile by his jealous rivals and died in Kyūshū. Subsequent misfortunes that befell the Kyoto court were attributed to Michizane's vengeful spirit.

[4] Taira no Masakado 平 将門 (d. 940) was a military commander who rebelled against the Kyoto government and died in battle. As with Michizane, many subsequent misfortunes were attributed to his vengeful spirit.

childish and *pre-modern* notion that their lives are governed by the gods or the curse of ancestral spirits.

I have already made it clear that Buddhists do not reject ancestral veneration out of hand. Mahāyāna Buddhism in China, before it ever came to Japan, had assimilated various practices in this line. This is a topic that merits study on its own, but suffice it here to note that the Buddha Dharma preached by Śākyamuni was a religion that originally had no relation with such practices.

A brief word about the two remaining elements, patronage and healing, both of which have to do with "worldly benefits." The followers of New Religions emphasize the practice of service to one another. Suppose, for example, that the owner of a bakery joins a New Religion. All of the members in the neighborhood, as well and many members who live further away, will come and buy their bread at that bakery. The material benefits that accrue for the new member are immediately evident. Many from traditional Buddhist schools look on such practices with scorn and find such appeals to worldly benefits a base form of religion. But is this really fair? Suzuki Shōsan,[5] a Zen priest and member of the samurai class in the early Tokugawa period, once said that if the Buddha, Dharma, and Saṅgha are to be called the "three treasures" of Buddhism, they must live up to their name as *treasures* and be beneficial to those living in the world. His words merit attention. Indeed, I consider Shōsan's Zen a predecessor of the "lay Buddhism" of the New Mahāyāna.

The third common element, healing, refers not only to the inner healing that goes on in the believer's heart but also to the healing of society and the world, to social reforms that represent one of the major responsibilities facing religion. In all ages the ruling class has feared the appearance of new religions and been quick to suppress them. The critical role that the "new religions" have played

---

[5] On Suzuki Shōsan 鈴木正三 (d. 1655) see Winston King, *Death Was His Kōan: The Samurai Zen of Suzuki Shōsan* (Berkeley: Asian Humanities Press, 1986).

throughout history points to the function of religion as an *outsider* to the existing social system. Today's Buddhist establishment is too closely tied to the powers that be, serving only the interests of the privileged classes and growing ever more oblivious of its duty to strive to "heal society" at large.

THE "PROGRESSIVE" SERMONS OF THE BUDDHA

Once again my pen has run astray of the subject matter at hand. Let us return to the idea of causality and karmic retribution. The Buddha accepted the current idea of causality as a foundation from which to teach his own Buddhist philosophy. Simply because he borrowed from prevalent notions of karma does not mean that to be a Buddhist one has to believe in karmic causality through time or in the transmigration of the soul.

I am reminded of an elderly well-known Sōtō monk who visited my place of retreat and told me, "Akizuki-san, there are people around today who claim to be Buddhists and yet deny the idea of causality through past, present, and future. What should we do about this?" I answered, "But I don't even believe in the existence of the past, present, and future," I replied. He was speechless and stared at me dumbfounded.

There is a kōan in the Rinzai tradition which asks, "What is the past, present, and future?", and whose answer is, "Already, now, and later."[6] For the true person, one who lives for the sake of the true self in the here-and-now, the past and future are of no moment. It is only when one has forgotten the present and lost the meaning of the absolute Now that one begins to lament the past and dread the future. Even if one accepts the idea of causality and karmic retribution, this does not mean that one has to accept the existence of the past, present, and future.

[6] This is the "secret answer" to a kōan based on a passage in the *Vajracchedikā-prajñāpāramitā-sūtra* that "the past is unattainable, the present is unattainable, and the future is unattainable."

It is important to distinguish clearly between those teachings of the Buddha, on the one hand, which assumed the general idea of causality current at the time, and the unique teachings of the Buddha Dharma that critically re-examine and go beyond that idea, on the other. The idea of reincarnation is another instance of a belief that is not essential to Buddhism. It is possible to talk coherently of causality and karmic retribution and yet repudiate the idea of reincarnation through time.

Even if one were to deny the life and death of the Buddha 2,500 years ago, there is no denying the momentary birth and death of particular thoughts in daily life. At one moment we feel caught in a living hell, and then we sit down to meditate and we feel as if we had been transported to the heavens. Or again, you may be riding the train home and savoring the teachings of your master when all of a sudden someone steps on your foot and you fall headlong into the realm of the *asura*. The problem is how to get free of this cycle of momentary birth-and-death, how to make the Buddha Dharma come to life. In this regard, we need to appropriate the wisdom of Zen Master Bankei,[7] who taught that we should perfect the "unborn mind of the Buddha" and not allow it to be supplanted by the mind of hell, hungry ghosts, and beasts.

Buddhism speaks of the "progressive sermons" of the Buddha, by which is meant a theory of education according to which teachings are not to be given all at once but in stages, from the simplest to the most advanced, just as a child is helped to progress from kindergarten through elementary school, middle school, and high school, all the way to university. Accordingly, Buddhism begins by teaching the practice of charity, keeping the precepts, and being reborn in heaven. Next one is taught about the evil that results from cravings and desires, and the benefits to be gained from abandoning these desires. Finally, one is instructed in the distinctively Buddhist doctrines of the Four Noble Truths, twelvefold dependent co-arising,

---

[7] See *The Unborn: The Life and Teaching of Zen Master Bankei (1622–1693)*, trans. by Norman Waddell (San Francisco: North Point Press, 1984).

and the Noble Eightfold Path. Thus even though the Four Noble Truths represented the real aim of Śākyamuni's teaching, other ideas were deemed necessary as preparations for that final lesson.

I should like to conclude this chapter with a brief word about the lessons of the first stage. "Charity" has to do with giving alms or helping others (such as the monks or the poor). "Keeping the precepts" has to do with keeping the five injunctions against killing, stealing, licentiousness, lying, and drinking alcoholic beverages. "Being reborn in heaven" refers to the promise of a pleasant rebirth in the next life through the accumulation of good karma. This assumes that rebirth in a pleasant realm is desirable, and is one of the assumptions that goes along with the theory of karmic retribution common in Śākyamuni's time. No doubt it was a theme used by Śākyamuni himself as an expedient means to help adjust his doctrine to the capacity of the unlearned masses.

The important task that lies ahead for us today is to re-examine the message of Buddhism that was taught on the basis of these assumptions. In Zen terms: "What is the Great Meaning of the Buddha Dharma?" "What is the soul of Buddhism?"

6 What Did Śākyamuni Teach?

THE TRANSMISSION OF EARLY BUDDHISM

What, then, is the unique "Dharma" taught by Śākyamuni? Let us begin by relating a story recorded in the early Buddhist *Āgama* texts.

After Śākyamuni had completed the Way and become the Buddha, and after he had pondered the profound nature of his enlightenment, he considered entering the final extinction of *nirvāṇa* right then and there. So unfathomably deep was the enlightenment he had attained, he thought, that even if he were to try to teach the Dharma to others, they would not be able to understand. At that moment Brahman, the supreme God, appeared to the Buddha and said:

> There are some lotuses in the pond that manage to break through the surface of the water and bloom, and others that sink deep beneath the surface and never come to flower. But there are also some that grow to just below the surface, and with a little help can break through and bloom. You should preach the Dharma for the sake of these.

The Buddha accepted the exhortation from Brahman and first preached the Dharma to five of his former friends and associates. This sermon, which has since come to be known as the "Sūtra on the Turning of the Wheel of the Dharma," explains the teachings of the Middle Path and the Four Noble Truths.

This first turning of the wheel of the Dharma consists of two parts. The first explains the teaching of the Middle Path — that there are two extremes in this world, and that one should avoid both extremes. The first extreme is indulgence in sense pleasures, which is base, vulgar, foolish, and futile. The second extreme is preoccupation with inflicting suffering on oneself, which is no less vulgar and futile. The Buddha taught that he had become aware of the Middle Path by renouncing these two extremes. In so doing, he came to a level of insight and discernment that brought him peace, enlightenment, awakening, and *nirvāṇa*.

This Middle Path which the Buddha taught represents the noble way to enlightenment and is made up of eight components: correct views, correct thoughts, correct words, correct actions, correct livelihood, correct effort, correct mindfulness, and correct meditation. Together they represent Śākyamuni's uncompromising rejection of the two extremes of hedonism and asceticism.

The second part of this sermon concerns the Four Noble Truths:

1. The truth of suffering.
2. The truth of the origin of suffering.
3. The truth of the overcoming of suffering.
4. The truth of the way to overcome suffering.

Briefly put, the content of each of the Four Noble Truths is as follows: the noble truth of suffering means that birth is suffering, old age is suffering, disease is suffering, death is suffering. Meeting a hateful person is suffering, parting with a loved one is suffering, not to achieve one's desires is suffering. In short, everything that makes up the material and spiritual life of humankind involves suffering.

Birth, old age, disease, and death are known as the "four sufferings"; these, together with meeting a hateful person, parting with a loved one, being unable to attain one's desires, and the pervasiveness of suffering, are called the "eight sufferings."

The second noble truth states that the origin of suffering lies in the desire for pleasure in one form or another, and that the craving and delight that accompany this desire become the cause of continued rebirth. *Desire* here includes not only sensual desires but also the desire to live on in another life as well as the desire for annihilation.

Life is suffering, but this suffering is neither punishment from the gods, nor mere coincidence, nor a matter of fate. What is the cause of suffering, then? According to the theory of causality based on the idea of karmic retribution, suffering is the natural result of our desires. This is the truth of the origin of suffering.

In identifying "desire" as the cause of suffering, the Buddha called it a "passionate thirst" that may be compared to "someone with an unquenchable thirst looking for water." The theory known as "twelvefold dependent co-arising" assigns the basic fault to "fundamental ignorance" (delusion, the absence of wisdom or *prajñā*). While the basic meaning of the two terms is the same, *passionate thirst* locates the cause of suffering in the realm of the emotions or senses, while *fundamental ignorance* locates it in the realm of the intellect.

Passionate thirst is of three kinds: the desire of the passions for sense pleasures; the "passion for existence" or the desire for life which aims at staying alive at all costs, even if that means continuing in some other form after death; the "passion for non-existence," which desires annihilation or the cessation of one's life. This latter is the impulse to suicide, to settle one's accounts with life once and for all and take leave of existence altogether. Since suicide is only an evasion of suffering, however, it does not solve the problem of human suffering. Śākyamuni identified all these forms of passionate desire or "fundamental ignorance" as the origin of rebirth and the never-ending cycle of transmigration.

The third noble truth of the overcoming of suffering teaches that these desires can be completely quenched, cut off at the roots and discarded, and that one can be liberated from all attachment to them. The state in which these desires have been done away with is called *nirvāṇa*, a state that is likened to the snuffing out of a flame. This truth of the overcoming of suffering is often referred to as the "extinguishing" of suffering, but Mahāyāna prefers to think in terms of overcoming desires through self-control.

The fourth noble truth teaches the eightfold way to overcome suffering, which we have just referred to in connection with the Middle Path. Early Buddhist tradition organized the eight elements that make up the Noble Eightfold Path into the "triple learning" of Precepts, Meditation, and Wisdom.

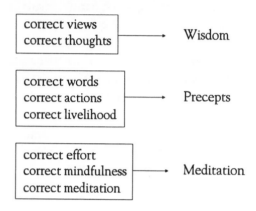

In monastic ordination, one "accepts the precepts" and thereby vows to live a regulated life. The practice of sitting in meditation (*zazen*) aims at stabilizing mind and body. Through these practices, one attains wisdom (*prajñā*) or enlightenment.

This, in short, is the teaching believed to have been taught directly by Śākyamuni. No doubt such an ordered account represents a compilation of the living teachings of Śākyamuni made shortly after his death and thereafter transmitted by his followers, the *saṅgha*, in the form of sūtras. In this way the Buddha Dharma of early Buddhism is often summarized in this form: the Four Noble Truths, twelvefold dependent co-arising, and the Eightfold Path.

Let us now consider the idea of "twelvefold dependent co-arising." It was only well after the time of Śākyamuni that the now familiar "twelve-link chain of dependent co-arising" was articulated theoretically. Just as Śākyamuni's doctrine of the Eightfold Path can be broken down into the simpler categories of Precepts, Meditation, and Wisdom, so the elements of dependent co-arising can be divided into delusions (ignorance), karma (actions), and suffering (distress).

The deluded state of "fundamental ignorance" leads one to perform karmic actions, which in turn brings the pain and sorrow of karmic retribution (the four and eight sufferings). This process follows the simple but fundamental law of causation:

> If this, then that;
> if not this, then not that.

The basic point of the theory of twelvefold dependent co-arising is that in order to eliminate suffering, one must purify one's karma or actions. In order to eradicate karmic retribution, one must awaken from the deluded state of fundamental ignorance and achieve true understanding (correct views). Since the doctrine of dependent co-arising was aimed at explaining the underlying intent of the Four Noble Truths, there is no need to cling to a theory of "causation through the past, present, and future" or the enumeration of a twelve-link process.

Śākyamuni understood that human suffering is the result of the thirst of passionate desires and ignorance. The control and quenching of this fire brings a state of *nirvāṇa*. But how does one go about attaining such a state?

If this, then that. There is ignorance, therefore there are the sufferings of birth, old age, disease, and death. *If not this, then not that.* If ignorance is annihilated, one can be liberated from human suffering. Śākyamuni came to realize this twofold causal process by practicing the extinction of ignorance and the control of the passions. In his quest for *nirvāṇa* he achieved enlightenment and awakened to wisdom (*bodhi*). It was from this perspective as an enlightened one that the Buddha taught the Four Noble Truths and its related doctrine of dependent co-arising.

THE BUDDHA'S SEARCH FOR LIBERATION FROM
THE CYCLE OF TRANSMIGRATION

In the foregoing we have had a brief look at the teaching of the Four
Noble Truths, which Buddhist scholars accept as the essence of the
Dharma taught by the historical Śākyamuni — or at least what that
essence was believed to be by the monks of the early Buddhist
saṅgha. I will reserve discussion of dependent co-arising for a later
chapter, but would now like to begin re-examining the background
to the Four Noble Truths from the perspective of the contemporary
world.

All the later developments of Buddhism — including early Buddhism, sectarian ("Hīnayāna") Buddhism, Mahāyāna Buddhism,
and so forth — are based on an "original Buddhism," that is, on the
teachings of Śākyamuni himself. In this sense the teaching of the
Four Noble Truths represents the essence of Buddhist thought. At
the same time, as I noted earlier, from the standpoint of New Mahāyāna, even this teaching is no more than *one form* of the Buddha
Dharma and not yet the fountainhead of the Buddha Dharma that
lies deep within the innermost recesses of what he was teaching.

The criticism has been made that "the Buddhist theory of the four
and eight sufferings is biased and one-sided."[1] Parting with a loved
one, it is said, is suffering. There is separation through death and
separation in life. There is the parting of lovers, and separations
which tear one apart like a majestic oak tree split down the middle.
To be sure such things are bitter and painful and full of suffering. At
the same time, parting entails that there was first a coming together.
What has never met, never separates. Unless one is prepared to say

[1] Akizuki is referring to a point made by the Christian theologian Yagi Seiichi
in a dialogue with Akizuki. Yagi is actively involved in the Buddhist-Christian dialogue movement, and has published widely in this area. In English one may refer
to the transcript of a theological encounter with Hans Küng and Francis Cook in
Buddhist-Christian Studies 9 (1989), and a review article in the same issue by
Odagaki Masaya, "An Introduction to the Religious Thought of Seiichi Yagi."

that being with one's loved ones is pain and sorrow, it would seem one-sided to speak only of suffering. If the parting is painful, then coming together with and being with loved ones is happiness. And there are many people in the world who live happy and joyful lives with those they love. Why single out the aspect of suffering? Isn't that a rather distorted view of human life?

As painful as it is to have to put up with offensive people or work with those one dislikes, it is still more painful to be all on one's own. In facing hardships, it is better to be with disagreeable people than to be left on one's own.

Similarly, no one will deny for a moment that it is painful not to get what one wants. But is it really desirable for all one's wishes to be fulfilled? Think for a moment about the "happy" boys and girls who are immediately given anything their little hearts desire. The fact is, it is often better *not* to get what one wants.

Or again, it is one of life's certitudes that those full of vigor and vitality are bound to suffer. But this is not necessarily an adversity, any more than birth, old age, disease, and death are. There are times when, in retrospect, one is thankful for having been subjected to an illness. There are many elderly people who live beautiful and fulfilling lives. Not all suffering is totally bad.[2]

There is undoubtedly much to be said for such criticisms. Unfortunately, however, it shows a lack of understanding of the true intent of the "truth of suffering" and the historical background out of which this idea emerged some 2,500 years ago. The Buddha's view of human life as suffering was shaped by the context in which people lived at the time, and in their context "suffering" referred first and foremost to the suffering of the cycle of birth and death.

What happens when someone dies? The question is one that concerns all human beings, past and present, East and West. Few people believe — or at least would prefer to believe — that death is a return to some absolute void. From time immemorial people have forged all

---

[2] See Yagi Seiichi's argument in a book he co-authored with Akizuki, 「般若心経」を説く *[Explaining the Heart Sūtra]* (Tokyo: Kōdansha, 1985).

sorts of notions about a realm of life after death. The same was true of ancient India.

The Upaniṣads teach that when people die they go to the next world, only to be reborn into this world. This cycle of birth and death, death and rebirth, continues without end. This is the idea known variously as transmigration, reincarnation, or metempsychosis. Whether one is born into a happy or an unhappy situation is a result of the actions (karma) of one's former lives. One's fate is sealed as a karmic retribution from one's deeds. Karma is the cause of transmigration. As noted earlier, this teaching of the Upaniṣads differed from the earlier idea in India that one's fortune or misfortune was determined by the will of the gods, and as such represents a more rationalistic idea based on a sense of self-autonomy. In any event, the theory of karmic causation was to dominate Indian philosophy for centuries to come.

Many believed that at death their spirit ascended into the sky along with the smoke from their cremated remains, passing along a dark path until it arrived at the world of ancestral spirits. From there their spirit was carried to the moon, whence it is returned to this world on the wind and the rain and is reabsorbed into the earth's vegetation. When the plants were eaten, the departed spirit would be assimilated into the body of the living and reborn through the male semen. Only a few chosen ones would follow the flames along the path of light to arrive at the realm of the gods, whence they would be transported through the sun to become one with the absolute Brahman. These "elect" are those who have cultivated the proper practices during their life and discovered the highest truth. They are the enlightened and liberated few who are not reborn. The ultimate identity of the self (*ātman*) and Brahman (the absolute, the highest principle of the universe, and the only true being) is the supreme truth of Upaniṣad philosophy.[3]

---

[3] This appears to be similar to Buddhist ideas, but is actually quite different. While Upaniṣads teach a unity of Brahman and the self, a "Great Self," Buddhism teaches that there is no ultimate self. The explanation of the process of life after

As long as people followed this primitive, childish belief that their happiness or misfortune depended on the will of the gods, their only recourse was to try and sway the designs of the gods through prayer and ritual. But once awakened to self-autonomy, to the idea that the fate of humankind depends on the actions of each individual (karma), and to the fact that the ideal measure of "good results for good deeds and evil results for evil deeds" does not work in the case of the individual human life, the ground was laid for the idea of karmic retribution through time, and the idea of suffering through transmigration in the six destinies.

In Śākyamuni's time, the idea that life (the cycle of birth and death, or *saṃsāra*) is suffering had to do primarily with the suffering of transmigration. The Buddha taught his Dharma principally as a way of liberation from the cycle of birth and death in these six destinies. We have touched on this in the former chapter, and there is no need to repeat it here. The main point is that, seen in this broader picture, the destiny of the human being — the destiny that you and I inhabit — is one of suffering, but not without certain pleasures.

Sentient beings pass through this cycle of birth and death with its six destinies over and over. They "transmigrate." If the span of a human life is only about seventy years, somehow or other we can manage to put up with it, despite the suffering. But this cycle of life and death was believed to continue on and on into an unbounded, unending future! No wonder the people of Śākyamuni's time shuddered with fear at the prospects of eternal rebirth. Was there no way to escape or be set free of this cycle? — this was the deep-seated human question that the religions of that time had to face.

Transmigration, then, was an accepted fact. There was no questioning the rule of karma. And insofar as Buddhism took shape as a response to longing for liberation from suffering in the present and the future, it could not but share the general religious context and

death is drawn from Watanabe Shōkō 渡辺照宏 , 仏教 *[Buddhism]* (Tokyo: Iwanami, 1956), 41-43.

certain of its assumptions with Jainism and the Ājīvikas,[4] despite its own distinctive teachings.

Given the possibility of countless lives of suffering awaiting them in the future, there were those who gave in to the pleasures of the senses. Others went to the opposite extreme, subjecting their bodies to ascetic rigors in anticipation of a future reward. Buddhism criticized both extremes of hedonism and asceticism, proposing in their place a middle way consisting of the Eightfold Path.

The Brahmin minority taught that there was an ultimate religious realm wherein the supreme God Brahman and the self of each individual were united. Unfortunately, this had nothing to do with the salvation of the masses. Nor did the traditional rituals performed by the priests or the prayers to the gods and spirits recited by the common people provide an answer to an age awakened to moral autonomy. It was into this gap that the Buddha stepped with his doctrine of the Four Noble Truths about the actual structure of human existence as consisting of suffering, the cause of suffering, the overcoming of suffering, and the path to effect that overcoming.

This completes our brief overview of the Buddha's teaching, but still leaves us with the question of what religious truth remains when we consider this teaching from our contemporary perspective. The Buddha saw life as suffering, he sought liberation from the cycle of life and death in order to escape rebirth in this world, and he spoke of this liberation as a state of eternal peace or *nirvāṇa*. In his quest for *nirvāṇa* he came to an unexpected enlightenment and wisdom (*bodhi*), which led him to his doctrine of the Four Noble Truths (and dependent co-arising). To consider what all of this can mean for our post-modern age, let us re-examine the basic teaching of Buddhism under the banner of the "New Māhāyana."

---

[4] Jainism and the teaching of the Ājīvikas were two religious movements in India contemporary with Śākyamuni. Jainism teaches that there is a sharp distinction between souls and matter, and that souls reincarnate through the force of karma. The Ājīvikas taught a kind of absolute determinism, that no amount of virtue or vice would affect the working out of one's karma.

7 In Search of the Foundations of Buddhism

THE LAW OF DEPENDENT CO-ARISING

The question "What is the Great Meaning of the Buddha Dharma?" appears commonly in Zen dialogues. The term *Great Meaning* does not refer to the outer structure of Buddhist teachings but to its inner core or essence. Its intent is to seek out the essential and basic Dharma (truth) taught by the Buddha. Ignoring for a moment what answer the Zen disciple might give to the question, let us begin with Śākyamuni's own answer: the Dharma of dependent co-arising. A famous story illustrates the point.[1]

Before joining ranks with the Buddha, Śāriputra and his friend Moggaliputta Tissa were renowned teachers with a hundred disciples each. They had been outstanding disciples of Sañjaya, a free thinker who came to be known in the Buddhist tradition as one of "the six teachers of heterodoxy."

Now it happened that Śāriputra once came upon a *śramaṇa* (wandering ascetic) begging in the town. The *śramaṇa's* face was pure and radiant, his appearance dignified, and his attitude irreproachable. Śāriputra thought to speak with him, but since it was not permitted to speak to a monk while he was begging, he followed after

---

[1] See Masutani Fumio 増谷文雄, 仏教百話 [*One Hundred Buddhist Stories*] (Tokyo: Chikuma Shobō, 1985).

the man until they were out of the town. He then approached him and asked, "Whose disciple are you?"

The śramaṇa, a disciple of the Buddha named Assaji, replied, "I am a disciple of the Buddha, Śākyamuni."

Śāriputra queried him further. "And what is the Dharma the Buddha teaches?"

Assaji responded with what have come to be known as the "verses on dependent co-arising":

> All dharmas arise through conditions;
> The tathāgata has taught these causes.
> His Dharma consists of dependent co-arising;
> This is the teaching of the Great Śramaṇa.[2]

Upon hearing these words, Śāriputra at once set out, together with his friend Moggaliputta Tissa, to become a disciple of Śākyamuni, and later became the Buddha's principal disciple.

Dependent co-arising is *the* representative teaching of Śākyamuni's Buddha Dharma, and as the legend of Śāriputra shows, was attributed to Śākyamuni already from the time of Early Buddhism.

Śākyamuni sought liberation from the suffering of life. He did not see human affliction as a punishment meted out by the gods for sin. Nor did he consider it a mere matter of chance or fate. His search for the root cause of human suffering finally led him to the conclusion that suffering is the natural result of human deeds (karma), and is subject to its own causes and conditions. This insight into the conditioning causes of suffering was the unique contribution of the Buddha:

> When there is this, there is that.
> When this arises, that arises.
> When this is not, that is not.
> When this disappears, that disappears.

---

[2] These "verses on dependent co-arising" are found in the Mahāvagga, a part of the Vinaya-piṭaka I). See *The Book of the Discipline*, vol. IV (Mahāvagga), trans. by I. B. Horner (London: Pali Text Society, 1982), 52–55.

As we have already explained in some detail, people in northern India at the time the Buddha lived had already broken free of the idea of the earlier Brahminic idea that fortune and misfortune are determined by the will of the gods. By the time Śākyamuni came on the scene, the belief that one's personal destiny is determined by one's own past deeds was widespread among the common people. Śākyamuni himself accepted this idea of karmic retribution and used it as his point of departure. The difference was that he spoke in terms of "causes and conditions" rather than of "causes and results," that is, he drew a distinction between direct causes and indirect conditions. The "cause" of a flower's growth and blossoming, for example, is inherent in the seed, but lacking the proper conditions, the seed cannot flower and bear fruit. Some years ago a Japanese archaeologist, Ōga Ichirō, came upon some lotus seeds in a vessel that had remained buried underground for thousands of years. When he planted the seeds and provided them with sufficient sun and water, he found that they grew into magnificent flowers. This is the working of causes and conditions which the Buddha taught accounts for the arising of all things.

THE MANIFESTATION OF THE DHARMA

Why is the answer to the question, "What did Śākyamuni teach?" that "He taught the Dharma of dependent co-arising" rather than "He taught the Dharma of the four truths"? The answer is simple: the teaching of the four truths *is* the Dharma of dependent co-arising. Besides the famous verses on dependent co-arising that we have cited in connection with the legend of Śāriputra, there is another famous set of verses on the Dharma of dependent co-arising that has come to attract great attention among scholars in recent years:

> The sage is absorbed fervently in his thought.
> When the myriad dharmas become clear
> His doubts completely disappear,
> Because he knows the Dharma of dependent co-arising.

The verses appear in a short sūtra from the Pāli canon known as the *Udāna*,[3] to which no full translation has been found in the Chinese canon. The phrase rendered above, in Masutani Sensei's translation, as *become clear* could also be translated *appeared*. Professor Tamaki Kōshirō, for example, translates the verses this way: "Truly the Dharma appears to the practitioner in ardent contemplation."[4] I myself prefer the phrase "becomes manifest," because "appearing" implies something visibly present before one's eyes, like the sun rising in the morning sky.

In any case, the question before us is, "What did Śākyamuni teach?" What was it that the Buddha realizes and was trying to put into words? What was the content of his enlightenment? These questions are crucial for understanding Buddhism. Laying out before me the versions of Masutani Sensei and Professor Tamaki, I must say — honestly, but not without some hesitation — that Masutani Sensei's handling of the text does not move me as much as Professor Tamaki's. Subtle though the differences are, they show Professor Tamaki for the true Buddhist scholar that he is, a man whose work is a realization of the Zen practice as a total engagement of the thinking person. The posture of his Buddhology is a model for what I mean by New Mahāyāna.

Although I have stated repeatedly that "Śākyamuni realized the truth of dependent co-arising" as it is found in so-called "primitive Buddhism," I cannot but register a certain uneasiness at my own insistence. For the idea of dependent co-arising is just one more ratio-

---

[3] For the standard Japanese translation, see the *Nanden daizōkyō* 南伝大蔵経 (Tokyo: Daizō Shuppan, 1971), vol. 23, 85–240.

[4] See Tamaki Kōshirō 玉城康四郎 , 仏教の根底にあるもの [*The Roots of Buddhism*] (Tokyo: Kōdansha Gakujutsu Bunko No. 731, 1986). Masutani acknowledges his own struggles in this regard: "For some reason I just could not get a grasp of what enlightenment is, and it frustrated me. But then at last I understood." See his 釈尊のさとり [*The Enlightenment of the Buddha*] (Tokyo: Kōdansha Gakujutsu Bunko No. 344, 1979), where he goes into great detail on the verses of the *Udāna*, both in the form in which they are cited in the text as well as variant prose versions.

nal theory, and it was surely *not* to some bone-dry theory that Śākya-muni awakened. What his eyes opened to was the "formless self," a realization of the "true person of no rank." This is what I take *satori* to be all about.

Permit me the indulgence of another personal reminiscence to make my point still more clearly. Towards the end of my graduate studies at Tokyo University, the prestigious chief administrator, who but rarely showed his face under the old system, came to me one day and asked, "Why don't you get on with it and finish your doctoral thesis? I see that you're pretty badly off and haven't the funds to pay your tuition, but we'll waive the examination fee. It's high time you and that Iwasaki [Takeo] fellow got a move on!" It wasn't as if I was waiting to be pushed, but his words helped me to make up my mind to go after the degree. I asked Professor Nakamura Hajime to be my adviser, but was turned down:

"A thesis written in the style of Suzuki Daisetz's scholarship won't pass at Tokyo University. Aren't there other places where this would be more welcome? Besides, I have my hands full of students just now."

Later, on my way back from the Matsugaoka Library, Miyamoto Shōson Sensei, who was walking with me, turned to me and said, "It's better for you to finish your study and get the doctoral degree. I already accepted Yamada Reirin's[5] thesis, you know!"

Looking back at Nakamura Sensei's statement that Suzuki Daisetz's style of scholarship would not pass muster at Tokyo University, I have to say that he did me a service by being honest about the state of affairs at the time. It is a testimony to the strength of Professor Tamaki's convictions that throughout his career at Tokyo University, where the ideal of scholarship adheres strictly to Ui Hakuju's stress on historical and textual studies, he was able to keep his academic work so thoroughly rooted in Zen practice. In considering his work a harbinger of the kind of Buddhist studies my "New

[5] Yamada Reirin 山田霊林 was chancellor of Komazawa University and later chief monk of the Sōtō temple Eihei-ji.

Mahāyāna" is aiming at, I mean also to voice a vehement protest against modern objective Buddhology. I can only offer a rousing applause for the sort of "total engagement of the thinking person" Professor Tamaki has championed, and hope that it will spread and flourish all the more.

TO LIGHT THE LAMP OF THE DHARMA
IS TO LIGHT THE LAMP OF THE SELF

To speak of the Dharma becoming manifest does not mean merely that the *principles* governing reality as a whole have come to light, but rather that karma has come to term and *true reality itself* shows itself to us. Śākyamuni did not just awaken to some ethereal *idea* of the Dharma as dependent co-arising, but to the living, warmblooded, "true person of no rank," the "formless self" in the flesh. This is why I keep insisting that *prajñā*, the wisdom of *bodhi*, refers to the "original purity of the mind."

When Śākyamuni spoke of his immediate experience, it was not in terms of a theory about dependent co-arising — that when there is this, there is that, and so forth — but of an original purity, a Buddha nature. My understanding of "Dharma" as referring to a self-awakening to an originally pure (empty and selfless) self is far from arbitrary. Indeed, it stems from a phrase attributed to the Buddha at the time of his death:

> The Tathāgata is departing. From now on let the Dharma
> be your light, let you yourself be your light.[6]

The Sanskrit word *dīpa*, translated into Chinese as "light," can also be taken to mean an "island" or "sand bar." The allusion in either case is to a place of safety for one about to be swept downstream in a mighty river, and thus the term can also be translated as *refuge*. "The Dharma is your island, your refuge."

It would seem sufficient to say that the Dharma was to be our

---

[6] See the *Mahāparinibbāna-suttanta*, the fifteenth work in the *Pāli Dīgha-nikāya*.

light. Why did the Buddha go on to add that we ourselves should be our own light? — Because the Dharma *is* our self, our formless self. Hence, when we are told to seek refuge in ourselves and rely on ourselves, it is our "formless self" as Dharma or Buddha-nature that is meant.

In the preface to *The Great Meaning of Buddhism*, a book that grew out of a series of lectures delivered to the Emperor and Empress immediately after the war, D. T. Suzuki wrote: "If there be four or five years of life still left in me, I would like to spend my final energies on writing a book in English on the fundaments of Buddhism."[7] Even though he was in fact to live for another twenty years, he was never able to see that task to completion. How, then, could someone like me expect to achieve what even Suzuki Daisetz could not? Still, that is a secret aspiration I share with my teacher and the task I have set myself from now on. For now, however, I would like to return to the theme of the Four Noble Truths to reconsider my understanding of the great significance of the way of Zen Buddhism.

A FOUNDATIONAL VIEW OF THE FOUR TRUTHS

Doctrinally speaking, it is more accurate to say that the Four Noble Truths represent the Dharma taught by Śākyamuni and that dependent co-arising simply supplied the underlying logic that supports it. But behind them both lay the awakening of the Buddha, the experience to which Buddhism traces its origins.

Śākyamuni, as we have already seen, sought liberation from the suffering of human existence (*nirvāṇa*) through yogic practice, and in the process — unexpectedly — awakened to *bodhi*-wisdom. As a result, *nirvāṇa* came to take on a meaning much wider than merely a quenching of the flames of passion and ignorance. It came to signify the very enlightenment or *satori* of the Buddha himself. As he cherished the joy of this *bodhi*-wisdom, he pondered his own awakening

---

[7] Spoken in the spring of 1947. See his 仏教の大意 [*The Great Meaning of Buddhism*] (Kyoto: Hōzōkan, 1947).

and finally sought to explain it to his former colleagues. This explanation became what are known as the Four Noble Truths, the content of which has been laid out in the previous chapter.

But if the fountainhead from which all Buddhist teaching springs is the awakening of Śākyamuni, it is all the more important for us to know exactly what it was that he realized in this experience. Not surprisingly, the scriptures do not provide us with details. *Satori*, after all, is not something that can be communicated with words. There is no way to understand it except to experience it directly, to realize it and become a Buddha oneself. This is the meaning of the phrase "Only a Buddha can transmit to a Buddha."[8] What *can* be said, however, is that in their attempt to describe the *satori* experience, the early Buddhist scriptures tell us that Śākyamuni's Dharma, the truth which he discovered and taught to his disciples, consisted of the truth of dependent co-arising. The problem is how to decide if this tradition is accurate or not.

All things arise through causes and conditions—if there is this, there is that; if there is not this, there is not that. There is ignorance, therefore there is the cycle of birth and death; if there were no ignorance, neither would there be any cycle of birth and death. Śākyamuni reflected on these two aspects of dependent co-arising in deep contemplation and entered a state of no-self. In that state he became oblivious to the self that is the root of all ignorance and passion. It was a state, we might say, of "absolute nothingness," a contemplation of formlessness.

In that state his eye came to rest on the morning star in the twilight of the sky. The sight of the star triggered an explosion of selflessness in the nothingness of contemplation and the wisdom of *prajñā* was made manifest. He had a direct insight into the original self, the original purity of the mind. This was the *satori* of Śākyamuni.

So that's what it's all about, this "original purity of the mind"! By

[8] See above, 24, n. 2.

nature, the mind — "the original self" — is pure and empty. Whether one has awakened to it or not, the *fundamental enlightenment* remains. The Buddha and sentient beings are a single, non-dual reality. As Hakuin says, "Sentient beings are originally Buddha."[9] Or in the words of Zen Master Lin-chi:

> On your lump of red flesh is a true person of no rank who is always going in and out of the face of every one of you [seeing with the eyes, hearing with the ears, thinking with the mind, and so on for the other vital functions]. Those who have not yet realized it [appropriated it into self-awareness], look! Look![10]

To put it yet another way, at the moment of awakening, Śākyamuni denied his ego and affirmed his self to become a true person who recognized both the negative and the positive aspects of emptiness and no-self. The follower of Zen says, "If there is no ego, then all is self." Earlier, in chapter 2, we cited the conjecture of Yamada Mumon Rōshi that when Śākyamuni saw the morning star and was awakened, he must have exclaimed, "Ah, I am twinkling." In more doctrinal and academic terms, the *rōshi* followed the example of Vimalakīrti and spoke of the "Dharma-gate of non-duality,"[11] likening the sky (emptiness) to the non-duality of self and others. As the saying goes,

> The heavens and I are of one root,
> All things and I are one body.

This means that I am not something separate from the rest of sen-

[9] From the opening line of his *Hymn to Zazen*. See above, 30, n. 7.

[10] From section 3 of the *Records of Lin-chi*. The translation is based on the translation by Ruth Fuller Sasaki, *The Recorded Sayings of Ch'an Master Lin-chi Hui-chao of Chen Prefecture* (Kyoto: Institute for Zen Studies, 1975), 3. The remarks in brackets are Akizuki's.

[11] One of the main themes of the *Vimalakīrti Sūtra* is "non-duality." See especially chapter 8, "Introduction to the Doctrine of Non-Duality," *The Teaching of Vimalakīrti*, trans. by Étienne Lamotte and rendered into English by Sara Boin (London: The Pali Text Society, 1976), 188-203.

tient beings, that all existence is integrated into a single, non-dual reality. In Buddhism, this is known as "the wisdom of equality," the opening of one's heart and mind to the wisdom of *satori*, the *prajñā* that sees the original purity (emptiness) of the mind. One who experiences and realizes one's "original self" in this way is a Buddha.

This is how I understand the Buddha's *nirvāṇa*-wisdom, the insight into extinction as awakening. The Eightfold Path was the way of practice he offered to reach this goal. Accordingly, I would propose that the "fountainhead of Buddhism" consists in this: that the Four Noble Truths are none other than an expression of a self-awareness of the original self. This means that the *pāramitā* (the *perfection* of what has been realized by appropriating it as one's own and living it out) of *prajñā* (the realization of the original purity of the mind) is the primary meaning of Buddhism.

In the Mahāyāna tradition, this idea of the "original self" evolved through the ideas of emptiness (*śūnyatā*) in the Mādhyamika school and consciousness in the Yogācāra school, to the theory of the "womb of the Tathāgata" (*tathāgata-garbha*) and the theory of Buddha nature, and was transformed into the Ch'an tradition in China, which is where we encounter Lin-chi's idea of the "true person of no rank." This is why it can be called the "fountainhead" of Buddhism.

How is this Buddha-nature or original self to be realized? This is where the practice of the "threefold learning" comes in. One who follows the way of Zen begins from the basic statement, grounded in firsthand experience of *satori*, that "If there is no ego, then all is self." When the ego is emptied and one has become non-ego, that emptying bespeaks a non-duality of self and others, a state in which "The heavens and I are of one root, all things and I are one body." At that point the sufferings of others become one's own sufferings, and a compassionate lament over the sufferings of others wells up of its own accord. This is the cry of compassion (*karuṇā*). Even if one becomes a Buddha, one cannot stay in *nirvāṇa*. The vow to be a bodhisattva and devote one's efforts to the salvation of the myriad of sentient beings is the natural outcome, the "wondrous practice," of enlightenment at work.

For me, this structure of awakening to true human existence forms the background to the doctrine of the Four Noble Truths. Such an approach helps illuminate the theory of dependent co-arising and keeps it from turning into dull, abstract doctrine. The moment one awakens to the realization that "If there is no ego, then all is self," and that emptiness means the non-duality of self and others, at that same moment one realizes that the dependent co-arising of all things represents the fundamental reality of human existence and human relationships, that all human beings are intimately related, and that one's own self and the selves of all others are bound inseparably to one another.

In this regard, we may recall the well-known analogy from the sermons of Śākyamuni himself:

> Friend, let us say that we have two bundles of reeds. When these two bundles of reeds lean on each other, they can stand up. In the same way, when there is this there is that. However, if one of these two bundles of reeds is taken away, the other bundle will fall to the ground. In the same way, if that is not, then this is not. If this is not, then that is not.[12]

In this simple analogy we get a glimpse of the incisive insight of the Buddha into the reality of human existence, the inseparability of the self and others.

For the Jewish philosopher Martin Buber, "In the beginning was the relationship." The Buddha's analogy of the bundles of reeds illustrates the truth that "while the I and the Thou are distinct, we can never be separate, and this is why I discover myself only in loving a Thou." Here we see the fundamental reality of human existence and the work of compassion (what Christianity calls *agape*) that underlies all of human existence. This principle of relationship was perceived through the Buddha's enlightenment as "dependent co-arising." In time, this idea of dependent co-arising would culmi-

[12] From the *Saṁyutta-nikāya*.

nate in the *Avataṃsaka Sūtra*, a text that Suzuki Daisetz has called the greatest systemization of Buddhist thought in the world.

Having had a brief look at the foundational principles of Buddhism, we draw one step closer to the task of forging a new Mahāyāna for our times.

8 The Buddha Dharma and the Zen Way

TRUTH IS ORIGINALLY CLEAR AND SIMPLE

"Simplicity is not the goal of art, but the closer one gets to the true meaning of something, the more one arrives at simplicity in spite of oneself." These are the words of Constantin Brancusi, a twentieth-century Rumanian sculptor (1876–1957) whose mystic life had a profound influence on many artists.[1]

When one passes one's sixtieth birthday, the years of searching and thinking — be it in the realm of art, philosophy, or religion — seem to congeal into a simple form. When Zen Master Lin-chi came to enlightenment, he shouted, "The Buddha Dharma of Ōbaku is not so complicated!" In more colloquial terms, we might render the famous phrase: "The teachings of my master Ōbaku do not amount to all that much!" This is not to say that he found Ōbaku's teachings worthless, but only that he saw the truth itself to be clear and simple, not complex and enigmatic.

In its original form, truth is the height of simplicity. Is it not often the case that people begin by twisting and bending the truth out of shape until it has become something complex, and then go through

---

[1] Quoted in "To Approach 'Truth' is to Come to Simplicity," *Asahi shinbun*, evening edition, 27 December 1986, 5.

all kinds of contortions to make their way back to its original simplicity? Anyway, this is how I find myself thinking of late.

And I am not alone. Zen Master Bankei never tired of preaching what he called the "Unborn Buddha Mind." Dōgen spoke of the "wonderful cultivation of original enlightenment." Hisamatsu Shin'ichi spoke of FAS Zen (Formless Self — All Humanity — Super-History). Takizawa Katsumi spoke of "the non-separable, non-identifiable, and non-reversible." D. T. Suzuki spoke of the logic of "identity and non-identity" ($A = non\text{-}A$, therefore $A = A$). Nishida Kitarō spoke of an "inverse correlation" and a "self-identity of absolute contradictories."

What Lin-chi spoke of as the "true person of no rank" (and Hisamatsu Sensei, as "formless self"), I like to envelop in the phrase

> In a single breath
> the transindividual individual.

In other words, religion is the self-realization of the original self, a life that is true to this original self. This is the conclusion I have come to after my many years of seeking on the Buddhist path. "In a single breath, the transindividual individual," is simply my way of paraphrasing the meaning of the "original self" in more precise and intellectual terms. It is no more than an attempt to explain the fact that the "true person of no rank" (the formless self) is not a "Great Self" but a "selfless self."

In order to spell out the simplicity to which my quest for the true essence of religion has led me, I would like briefly to reiterate the three tenets proposed by Shaku Jōkō Rōshi, which we introduced in chapter 2, and on which we can now elaborate from a wider perspective.

MAHĀPRAJÑĀPĀRAMITĀ

What is the true essence of Buddhism, the one thing without which Buddhism would not be Buddhism? The answer is *Mahāprajñāpāramitā*. The word is hardly part of ordinary language, and one might stare at it until doomsday without being able to make any sense of it. Only when we relocate the word in the context of the ancient Sanskrit language from which it derives does its meaning comes to life for us.

The first part of the word, *mahā*, means great, large, superior. The next two syllables, *prajñā*, means wisdom in the sense of a wisdom that surpasses both everyday common sense and scholarly learning, a wisdom that can only result from a religious awakening. Finally, *pāramitā* means completion or perfection. Thus *Mahāprajñāpāramitā* means "the perfection of superior wisdom."

The next step is to find out what *prajñāpāramitā*, "the perfection of superior wisdom," means, what awakening or *satori* is all about. "Buddhism" refers not only to the teaching of the Buddha but also to a teaching that shows how we, too, can become Buddhas, "those who have awakened," "enlightened ones." In other words, the true essence of Buddhism is *prajñā*, the realization of enlightenment.

Up until the end of the Second World War, the term *prajñā* was thought to have been introduced by the Mahāyānists around the beginning of the Common Era, a few hundred years after the death of the Buddha. After the War, however, Nishi Giyū of Tōyō University published research demonstrating that the word was already in currency at the time of Śākyamuni when it meant "the original purity of mind" or "the self's original nature."[2] We have already pointed out affinities between the notions of purity, emptiness, and *prajñā*.

With the help of Shibayama Zenkei Rōshi's[3] commentary on Hakuin's *Hymn to Zazen*, these verses can serve as a valuable introduction to Hakuin's Zen. Hakuin opens his collection with the phrase "Sentient beings are originally Buddhas." That is, sentient beings — all living, unenlightened things — are originally or inher-

---

[2] The reference is to Nishi Giyū, *Studies on "Prajñā" in Primitive Buddhism.* See above, 26 & n. 3.

[3] Shibayama Zenkei 柴山全慶 (1894-1974) was former abbot of Nanzen-ji in Kyoto and taught at Hanazono and Ōtani universities.

ently "Buddhas." The statement recalls the famous verse repeated
throughout the *Nirvāṇa Sūtra* that "All sentient beings have the
Buddha nature," as well as the passage from the *Engaku-kyō* that
"Sentient beings are inherently Buddhas."[4] Here we have one of the
foundational ideas of Mahāyāna Buddhism. But it is not only a part
of the Mahāyāna tradition. It goes back to the enlightenment of
Śākyamuni himself from which all Buddhism began.

In his *Zazen wasan*, Hakuin speaks of "the immediate realization
of one's nature," of "opening the gates to where cause and effect are
one," and closes with the statement that "this body itself is Buddha."
The term *cause* in this context means sentient beings, or those who
are still at the stage that they need to be "caused" to realize Buddhahood; *effect* refers to the resultant realization of Buddhahood. The
oneness of cause and effect is thus synonymous with the "the non-
duality of sentient beings and Buddhahood" and the idea that "sentient beings are inherently Buddhas."

For Hakuin, then, the heart of Buddhism lies in the self-realization of the oneness of cause and effect, that is, in the original self.
The famous verse describing Zen speaks of it as

> Pointing directly to mind,
> Seeing one's [true] nature and attaining Buddhahood.

The words *mind* (or "heart") and *nature* are meant to point to the
"originally pure" Buddha nature, the basic nature of all beings which
is inherently possessed of Buddhahood. This is what I mean by the
term *original self.*

Thus the term *awakening* in Buddhism implies the self-realization
of an inherently pure original self, and this is the meaning of *prajñā.*
The opening of the mind's eye and clear perception of the basic nature of one's self is also what Hui-neng circumscribed by the term
kenshō ("perceiving one's nature"). In this regard we may mention
Hui-neng's celebrated verse, traditionally believed to illustrate the
difference between the Southern School of Ch'an Buddhism and

---

[4] 円覚経 , Chin., *Yüan-chüeh ching.* See T 842, 17.915-92.

the Northern School, and note its sharp contrast to the verse of Shen-hsiu, which symbolizes the latter line of tradition. First Shen-hsiu:

> The body is the Bodhi tree,
> The mind is like a clear mirror.
> At all times we must strive to polish it,
> And must not let the dust collect.

Here the mind is likened to a looking-glass that must continually be wiped clean and kept free of defilement. This is not an unsophisticated view, but it remains in the realm of moral cultivation.

Next consider Hui-neng's verse, which reads:

> Originally there is no tree of enlightenment,
> Nor is there a stand with a clear mirror.
> From the beginning not one thing exists;
> Where, then, is a grain of dust to cling?[5]

Hui-neng's words point to a mental realm of inherent purity where there is originally nothing at all to be defiled. They are like a finger pointing directly to the naturally pure mind.

In line with the difference between the two poems, Shen-hsiu's Northern School of Ch'an came to be known as the school of "gradualistic practice," stressing as it did the gradual purification of the mind through the cultivation of various practices. Meantime, Hui-neng's Southern School was called the school of "sudden awakening" in which the immediate realization of the originally pure nature of the mind was stressed. This latter school pursued the radical truth of the Zen of the patriarchs to which the Zen saying refers:

> All at once, in a single bound,
> Into the realm of the Tathāgata."[6]

---

[5] Cited from H. Dumoulin, *Zen Buddhism: A History* (New York: Macmillan, 1987), vol. 1, 132-33.

[6] From the 永嘉集 *[Hymns on the Path to Enlightenment]* compiled by Hsüan-

Thus has "Zen" come to pride itself on representing the central tradition of Buddhism as a way to gain direct experience of the awakening of Śākyamuni. For Zen, there is no Buddhism without the *satori* of "sudden awakening." In this sense, Zen is not just one school of Buddhism among many. It is the alpha and omega of Buddhism. As the common saying goes, "Zen encompasses all of Buddhism." For without the Zen insight into the identity of *samādhi* and *prājña*, and the unity of Meditation and Precepts, Buddhism would not be Buddhism at all.

In his declining years, during the course of a discussion with Yagi Seiichi, Hisamatsu Sensei exclaimed, "I am without *bonnō* (defiling passions)."[7] Yagi reacted to the apparent arrogance of the statement by noting that if this meant that Hisamatsu Sensei was speaking at that moment from the "cognitive perspective" of the individual who transcends individuality, then he could well understand what he was trying to say. For me, this is precisely the problem.

In theory, of course, there is nothing wrong with drawing a distinction in the "individual who transcends individuality" between the two aspects of the "transcendent individual" and "individuality." But while it is acceptable to speak from a *cognitive perspective* of an individual transcending individuality, from an *existential perspective* it is altogether out of place. I have to wonder if Yagi was aware of this. Perhaps the oversight is to be expected from a Christian point of view. But for Zen, which insists that the only thing that truly exists is "In a single breath, the transindividual individual," there is no such thing as a simple "individual" or "transindividual."

It is not that I mean to question the profundity of Hisamatsu Sensei's experience of awakening, but neither can I simply ignore the strong criticisms that the two *rōshi*, Morimoto Shōnen[8] and

---

chiao 玄覚 in the T'ang period. See T 48.396a18.

[7] See Hisamatsu Shin'ichi and Yagi Seiichi, 覚の宗教 [*The Religion of Satori*] (Tokyo: Shunjūsha, 1986.

[8] Morimoto Shōnen 森本省念 (1909-1984) was superintendent of the Naga-oka Zen Society and was successor to Yamazaki Daikō as head of the Shōkoku-ji

Shibayama Zenkei, raised against what he said. From the existential standpoint of the self in the here and now, how can one get away with making the claim, "I am without *bonnō*"? Along with Zen Master Jōshū,[9] who once said, "I experience defiled passions for the sake of all sentient beings," I am not as ready as Yagi seems to be to conclude that statements like that of Hisamatsu are spoken from the perspective of one who has transcended individuality. This brings us to the second of Shaku Jōkō's tenets.

PRECEPT, MEDITATION, WISDOM – THE UPHILL PATH AND THE DOWNHILL PATH

Prajñā, then, is a realization of the inherently pure nature of the original self. In Japan it was Zen Master Bankei who taught this doctrine in its most extreme form. For Bankei, all things are subsumed into an "Unborn Buddha Mind," which all people are born with but forget about in the course of filling their minds with mere "thoughts." If one gives in to covetous thoughts, he taught, one takes on the mind of a hungry ghost; to spiteful thoughts, the mind of a fighting demon. If one is without shame and always complaining, one will have the mind of a beast. Bankei did *not* make the claim that he had eliminated all such thoughts in himself. He never said he was "without defiling passions." He was a man of immense compassion and great wisdom, and for that I admire him and hold him up as a model of the perfection (*pāramitā*) of wisdom (*prajñā*).

Perfecting wisdom is important, and in this regard the Zen studies of Hisamatsu, which point directly to the inherent purity of the original self, are impressive. But in concentrating on the great task of pointing to this original purity, is he not a cut below Shibayama and Morimoto in the other great task of "cultivating practices for enlightenment"?

branch of Rinzai Zen.

[9] Chao-chou Ts'ung-shen 趙州従諗 (778–897), the disciple of Nan-ch'üan and protagonist of the bizarre Zen story in which he puts his sandal on his head upon hearing that his master killed a cat. See Dumoulin, *Zen Buddhism* 1, 167.

Prajñā must be perfected. The *original*, innately pure self must be actualized and completed as a *real* ego. This is where the second of the three tenets — the cultivation of Precepts, Meditation, and Wisdom — comes into play.

For all its talk of *prajñā* as "the nature of the mind as inherently pure," Buddhism is not only a philosophy but also a religion. The inherently pure mind must be experienced in an immediate and personal manner, and this leads us to an important qualification. *Pure* is not meant here as the opposite of what is "defiled." It is meant to point rather to an *absolute purity* that Mahāyāna Buddhism calls "emptiness." The practice of Buddhism begins with the experience of emptiness — of a self empty of all independence and self-sufficiency. This experience is called *samādhi*, a Buddhist form of yogic experience.

From its earliest days, Buddhism advanced a "threefold learning" as essential for all Buddhists, whatever their state in life. The learning begins with the Precepts, which are intended to assist one in the regulation of daily life according to Buddhist principles. A properly regulated life assures the control of body and mind needed to proceed to the second realm of learning, Meditation or *samādhi*. Zazen is often referred to as the ordering and regulation of the spirit, but it is more correct to see it as a harmonious disposition of body and mind. In *samādhi*, the whole body-and-mind is in order and at peace. In this state, the ego becomes empty and one is brought to the third element in the threefold learning, Wisdom awakened to selflessness. The point I wish to stress here is that it is only by emptying the self — that is, only through the experience of *samādhi* — that this realization of the original, selfless self is possible.

Śākyamuni began his quest for enlightenment by submitting himself to ascetical practices. Once he realized that asceticism alone would never bring him to his goal, he took up the practice of a form of yoga. Through a profound yogic experience, he succeeded in emptying himself of self and arriving at the selfless self. This was his *bodhi*, his awakened *satori*.

By keeping the Precepts, practicing *samādhi*, and experiencing *sa-*

tori, Buddhists seek to imitate the example Śākyamuni set. The path as we have just described it, proceeding from Precepts to Meditation and from Meditation to Wisdom, is known as the "uphill" path, and is still *pre*-Buddhist. True Buddhism begins only when one has turned back to the "downhill" path that proceeds from the realization of Wisdom back through Meditation and the keeping of the Precepts.

The way "downhill" involves what Dōgen calls the "wondrous practice of original enlightenment." Here *prajñā* Wisdom leads to a natural fulfillment of the first five *pāramitā*: charity, keeping the Precepts, patience, diligence, and Meditation. Whereas in the Indian context we may speak of Meditation (*samādhi*, *zen*) as one-third of the threefold learning, in China it is really "one-oneth" of the Buddhist doctrine. As Hui-neng, the Sixth Patriarch, says, "*Samādhi* and Wisdom are the same, *zen* and the Precepts are one." This is why I would insist that for Zen, Meditation is "one-oneth" of the Buddhist way.

Along with Śākyamuni, then, Hui-neng saw that the essence of *satori* lay in the "self-awareness of the original self" (*prajñā*) and that the perfection of other virtues follow as the *spontaneous self-unfolding of wisdom* in daily life, that is, they are the "*pāramitā* of *prajñā*," the one final Great Matter of Buddhism.

Dōgen speaks of the "correct transmission of the supreme Buddha Dharma."[10] One of the basic tenets of Dōgen's thought, the "wondrous practice of original enlightenment," is synonymous with what I have called the "spontaneous self-unfolding of *prajñā* in *pāramitā*." This is the quintessence of the Zen of everyday life. "Noble deeds are the Buddha Dharma, doing the Dharma is the heart of the teaching."[11] Dōgen's followers, however much lip-service they paid to "just sitting," in practice regressed to the *zazen* of ignorant fools, a kind of fanciful illusion or waking sleep. Similarly, those who fol-

---

[10] The term appears in the "Discourse on Practice" chapter of the *Shōbōgenzō* (see above, 30, n. 6).

[11] A common Zen saying whose source we were not able to trace.

lowed the teachings of Bankei, the purest form of T'ang China Zen
that came closest to the teaching of Śākyamuni's Buddha Dharma,
slipped into an innocuous Zen even as they went around speaking of
the Unborn Buddha Mind.

Hakuin saw through what was going on and raised a harsh voice
of protest against the epigons of Dōgen and Bankei. Indeed, this was
what gave Hakuin's Zen its special quality. At first encounter, one
might think that his idea of religion belongs to a different dimension
from that of Dōgen and Bankei, but in fact quite the exact opposite
is the case. As we have seen, Hakuin championed the idea of "oneness of cause and effect" by teaching that "sentient beings are originally Buddha." This has led some popular Zen commentators to the
myopic conclusion that "Dōgen's Zen takes the downhill path and
Hakuin's the uphill path." One could hardly be more wrong about
the essential nature of the Zen of these two masters. Hakuin was a
"Protestant" in Japanese Zen.[12]

THE SHEER, UNATTACHED MIND OF GREAT COMPASSION

My esteemed teacher D. T. Suzuki once criticized contemporary
Zen for being "too preoccupied with *prajñā*-wisdom to the neglect of
the practice of the most important element of the Buddha
Dharma — compassion." Elsewhere he remarked that "The Pure
Land of bliss is not a place where one goes to stay put. As soon as
you get there, you must return at once to this land of suffering to
share in the tribulations of sentient beings." For Suzuki Sensei, all of
Zen revolved about "the sheer, unattached mind of Great Compassion." That is, he was convinced that the fulfillment of the bodhisattva vows was the quintessence of Buddhism. "The four universal
vows — those are my *satori*," he said.[13]

In a similar vein, Dōgen says that "The aspiration for enlighten-

---

[12] For further elaboration, the reader is referred to my *Zen Master Hakuin*. See
above, 30, n. 8.

[13] The quotations in this paragraph are actually Akizuki's paraphrases of statements frequently made by Suzuki.

ment (*bodhicitta*) is the commitment to help others cross to the
other shore (of enlightenment) before one has crossed over oneself."[14] He likened himself to a "ferryman who carries one person
over after the other, without getting off himself."[15] No sooner has
the bodhisattva delivered someone to the realm of awakening than
he turns back to this world, never stopping to take up abode on the
yonder shore. This is the sense of the universal vow "However innumerable sentient beings, I vow to save them all."

The idea of a sheer, unattached mind of Great Compassion is not
simply a paraphrase of the goal of "saving even sentient beings with
whom one has no connections." It is an absolute compassion, so
great as to break through all bounds of who, what, where, when, and
how.

How is such an absolute, unlimited compassion possible? Where
can such an unattached mind of compassion spring from? Where, indeed, if not from the perfection of *prajñā*, the self-awakening of the
original self! This is why I insist on locating *prajñā* in *satori*, where
"wisdom and compassion are one," and why I explain *samādhi* as the
practice of emptying the self.

Awakening to the original self is a religious experience mediated
by a self-emptying or negation of the ego. Referring to the passage in
the *Diamond Sūtra* which says that "the self is not a self, therefore it
is called self,"[16] Suzuki Sensei introduced what he called the "logic
of *and/not*."[17] The more the ego is emptied and negated, the more
the original self is made manifest — this is the dialectic of emptiness.

In the previous chapter mention was made of the saying, "If there
is no ego, all is self." Suzuki Sensei had the same thing in mind when
he spoke of a "zero-in-infinity." At the moment of emptiness, the

---

[14] From the 発菩提心 "Awakening of the *Bodhi*-Seeking Mind" chapter of the
Shōbōgenzō.

[15] Akizuki is here citing a well-known Japanese Buddhist poem.

[16] See Edward Conze, *Buddhist Wisdom Books* (New York: Harper Torchbooks,
1972).

[17] 即非の論理.

zero-point of selflessness, all sentient beings are the self. Self is at once oneself and other selves. It is, in Hisamatsu Sensei's terms, a "formless self." Because awakening to the emptiness of the ego is the spontaneous, self-unfolding of the original, formless, empty self itself, at the moment of awakening the sufferings of other selves become the sufferings of one's own self, and consciousness of the karuṇā — com-passion — is set in motion. This is sheer, unattached Great Compassion. This is the "Unborn Buddha Mind" of Zen Master Bankei.

Perhaps the one human psychological state that comes closest to this Buddha-mind is maternal love. When she holds her infant in her arms, the mother is emptied of all ego. The relationship between the two is a "non-duality of self and other." When her baby has a stomach ache, it is as if the mother's own stomach ached. Because these feelings are a matter of instinct and not something refined through a cultivation of the threefold learning of Precepts, Meditation, and Wisdom, they quickly fall by the wayside as time goes on. If one's child gets in a fight with another child, an educated mother will scold her child, "Stop that nonsense!", even though she knows in her heart that her child is in the right and the neighbor's child at fault. Śākyamuni's saying, "These three worlds [of desire, form, and formlessness] are my existence; all who live in them are my children"[18] reveals a profound understanding of "emptiness" as the "non-duality of self and others."

Anyone who claims to have experienced satori and yet does not feel the suffering of the young starving in Ethiopia, cannot be said to embody the true "non-duality of self and others." For this was precisely what the Buddha meant by satori. When the originally pure mind of prajñā lives in such a self, it is not enough to say "I am without defiling passions." My primal vow must rather be, "Even though my days of vain nihility come to an end, this my heart's desire will never be exhausted."

By this time, you may be thinking to yourself, "Whatever this fel-

---

[18] The passage appears in the Kegon (or Avataṃsaka) Sūtra.

low is trying to say, surely it isn't nearly so clear and simple as he makes it out to be. It sounds like just one more complicated sermon to me." But for me the Buddha Dharma is nothing so enigmatic. It all comes down to this: The Buddha Dharma means awakening to the selfless self in which there is a non-duality of self and others — the original self for which "when there is no ego, all is self" — and living within that awareness. This original self is realized in the denial of the ego — that is, in *samādhi* — and there it is lived. In a life of egolessness, one does not measure everything in terms of oneself. Rather, one seeks to live out of the sheer, unattached mind of Great Compassion for the sake of one's neighbor. As complicated as it must all sound when set out in theoretical terms, in practice it can all be summed up in one word: Jōshū's "*Mu*"![19]

Mahāprajñāpāramitā!

---

[19] The allusion is to the short opening case of the *Mumonkan*. Asked by a monk whether the dog has a Buddha-nature, Jōshū barks back at him, "*Mu*" — Nothingness! See above 95, n. 9 and 55, n. 12.

Responding to Today's World

9 Zen, Medical Science, and the Post-Modern World

MEDICINE FOR A POST-MODERN AGE

The way of medicine has important affinities to the way of the Buddha. After all, a doctor's work is to deliver people from the pain of birth, old age, illness, and death. Insofar as saving patients from these four sufferings is what medical practice aims at, then all doctors cannot but have fundamental ties to the Buddhist path.

Tradition calls Śākyamuni "the great doctor-king." His sermon on the Four Noble Truths, as we have already explained, begins from the sufferings of life, seeks their underlying cause, probes into the original state of human being, and takes practical measures to achieve its restoration. The Buddha Dharma is root and branch a way for saving people. A moment's reflection should suffice to show that things are no different for medical practice. Doctors follow a way of therapy that also diagnoses illness, seeks out its causes, and works to restore the sick to a state of good health. All doctors, even if they do not happen to be *great* doctor-kings, at least try to be *small* ones.

During my fifties, I lectured on ethics and religion at Saitama Medical University. Throughout my lectures I had but one thing in mind and repeated it over and over in a variety of forms. In effect I told my students:

At the roots of the Western medicine that you are studying lies a modern Western view of what it means to be
human. And *that* is the problem. The humanism of modern
bourgeois society that underpins Western medicine rests on
what the history of philosophy calls "awakening to the ego."
Compared with the view of the human in medieval feudalism
and in the quasi-feudalism whose remnants survive up to the
present, there is no denying that this standpoint has borne
spectacular and dazzling results for the human race. But
what if it should turn out that this vigorous modern view of
the human that we call modern humanism is infected with
what Kierkegaard calls a "sickness unto death"? Would we
not have to reexamine the notion of the "modern ego" un-
dergirding Western medicine? That is why we need to have
another look at the "oriental mind" preached by the Buddha,
the so-called "Buddha-mind" that has been passed down
from generation to generation in our country since the time
of Prince Shōtoku.

Throughout my ten years at Saitama Medical University, a single
question preoccupied me in my teaching: *If medicine's basic view of
the human is in error, what kind of medicine can it be?* Somehow I could
not help thinking there was a basic ignorance (*avidyā*), coupled with
a lack of education in what it means to be awakened to the one and
only indispensable wisdom (*prajñā*), that had allowed a fundamental
mistake to creep into contemporary medical science. Alas, my concerns did not become an issue at Saitama Medical University itself.
But when I later received positive feedback from Tsuchiya
Kensaburō, President of the Industrial Medical University, I was relieved that an important figure in the world of medical education
seemed to have understood what I was trying to say.

The Meiji intellectuals who set out to reshape Japan in the last
century followed the European model of modernization. For the last
hundred years we have been blessed with the fruits of that process.
Despite the miserable state to which we were reduced at the end of
the War in 1945, the fact that a spectacular economic recovery has

taken place to elevate Japan to the ranks of the leading countries of the free world is no doubt due in large part to that modernization. (Still, let it be said, it pains the heart to face the fact that to a certain degree our "rapid growth" in the post-War years took place under the nuclear umbrella of the United States and over the tortured vic-tims of Korea and Vietnam.) And when one further considers the fact that the neighboring People's Republic of China, which was supposed to have already had its socialist revolution under the lead-ership of Mao Tse-tung, today, with Deng Hsiao-ping at the helm, is going all out in the direction of modernization, it is hard not to con-clude that modernization is the only way for the human race to go, and that after all we owe a profound debt of gratitude to those who have promoted it since the Meiji era.

Already in the 1840s, however, there was a group of people with the insight to realize, from within their European homelands, that human history had already begun to shift from the *modern* world to a *contemporary* one. Their realization took shape in a critique of Hegelian philosophy, the crowning philosophy of the modern world. One such critique was the existentialist movement that began with Kierkegaard and was carried on by Nietzsche and others. Another current passed over from Ludwig Feuerbach's materialistic anthro-pology to the communism of Karl Marx. Kierkegaard and Marx — the one a Christian, the other an atheist — might seem to many to be standing back to back and headed in opposite directions. But their common conviction of "the end of the modern world," spoken with a sensitivity to the philosophy of history like that of Old Testament prophets, and the way in which both of them saw the reality of the post-modern world as the historical destiny of the human race, oblige us to see them as thinkers of common sympathies.

On reflection, Japan also had its thinkers who bucked against the frenzied spirit of Europeanism that seemed to have a stranglehold on the popular imagination (as symbolized in institutions like the Rokumei-kan).[1] While some of those who resisted were simply

---

[1] The Rokumei-kan 鹿鳴館 was a center built in 1881 to promote moderniza-

anachronistic bigots, there were others of deeper insight who were able to roll with the punches as they worked to construct a new image of what it means to be human, an image that would take them beyond modernity. Some of these latter were able to step into the van of Japan's modernization without ceasing to reject those elements in Western civilization to which they did not wish to adapt, but also without failing to take adequate stock of what was good in modernity. I find Natsume Sōseki and his literature representative of just such a posture.

In one of Sōseki's novels, the protagonist is made to exclaim, "Nothing stands in my way to regulate me."[2] But as we watch him try to live as an enlightened "modern," we see the "quasi-feudalistic Meiji emperor system" plant its feet firmly in the way of his advance. The ideal of absolute imperialism chokes the life out of his enlightened ego. At the same time, his traditional upbringing as a Japanese and an Oriental resists modern Western civilization's image of the human. Through the person of his character, we see Sōseki searching for a post-modern image of the human that will accept what is of value in modernity and yet move beyond it.

I myself am persuaded that a contemporary, post-modern view of the human can be forged from the Mahāyāna idea of *śūnyatā*, or emptiness, an idea that is fundamental to Zen and its idea of an original *anātman*, or egolessness. Given Sōseki's lifelong devotion to Zen, I would like at some future date to return to the question of how Sōseki arrived at a view of the human that forecasts the emergence of the post-modern individual.

THE PROBLEM OF PSYCHOSOMATIC MEDICINE

After the Second World War, a new movement in the medical world

tion during the Meiji and Taishō periods, and soon became a symbol of the era's relentless drive for Westernization.

[2] Natsume Sōseki 夏目漱石 (1867-1916) was the premier novelist of the Meiji Period. The novel referred to here is *And Then*, translated by N. M. Field (New York: Putnam, 1982).

grew up in the United States under the name of "psychosomatic medicine." The movement is said to be a godchild of the psychoanalytic revolution of Freud and Jung. Psychoanalysis had already demonstrated scientifically how illnesses that had previously been thought of only in terms of physical disorder in fact come under a strong and deep influence of the psyche and its unconscious processes. Depth psychology also showed that it was able to effect lasting therapeutic results for certain kinds of illness without the use of physical medicine. This in turn led to a rethinking of the way in which modern Western medicine had lost sight of the whole person and cut off an important dimension of being human. Criticism was raised against the mistaken bias of medical science that healing means treating the human being only at the lowest level of the flesh, as something animal, material, and mechanistic. Already some forty years ago in the United States the medical world was being called to task for its failure to recognize a fundamental distinction between what is human and what is merely organic. The questions shook medical science at its foundations and faced the philosophical and intellectual world with questions of great moment. This critical mood survives today in efforts being made to construct a suitable theory of the "body."

Illnesses of the mind that cannot be cured by medication alone and ailments of the body whose causes lie in the mind are widespread among contemporary men and women. There is even a name for it: "psychosomatic disorder." As Professor Ishikawa Hitoshi of Tokyo University has noted, "It is a state of disease whose main symptoms are physical but whose diagnosis and cure make it particularly important to take into account the mental element." Over half of the cases of so-called adult illness — high blood pressure, stenocardia, ulcers, rheumatism — are said to fall into this class.

With all the stresses in modern society, such maladies tend to increase. But they are not like the sort of infection that can be treated by killing bacteria with medication or surgical removal. Their healing requires the self-control of the sufferer. This is why psychosomatic medicine proposes various "methods for autonomic control," among which yoga and *zazen* have been widely adopted.

The pioneer of psychosomatic medicine in our country is Ikemi Yūjirō, Professor Emeritus of Kyūshū University, where very early on he set up a Department of Psychotherapeutic Internal Medicine within the Medical Faculty. Currently he is recognized as one of the world leaders in the International Association for Psychosomatic Medicine. I quote Professor Ikemi's own words:

> I have spent fully half a lifetime in the field of psychoso-
> matic medicine. Through the grace of exchange with first-
> rate scholars at home and abroad, I have tried to search
> through the wisdom of the East to find out what I can about
> understanding the human being as a total person, and what
> methods of self-control there are based on such an under-
> standing. I have found that Zen represents a crystallization of
> the wisdom of the East about self-control, and it is now my
> unabashed conviction that the simplest and clearest method
> of pure self-control available to all is *zazen*, and in particular
> the "just sitting" of Dōgen.[3]

Here we may pass over the idea of Zen as a "pure method of self-con-trol" or the "just sitting" of Dōgen to which Professor Ikemi alludes. The important point is that medicine alone does not suffice to check the diffusion of mental illness or psychosomatic disorders in our day. But neither are the illnesses of the contemporary age merely a prob-lem that calls for therapies of self-control and the like. The problems and solutions announced by psychosomatic medicine, as Professor Ikemi says, require a much more basic change, a transformation of perspective of our view of the human.

One of the cornerstones of modern Western medicine is the mind-body dualism that has been current in one form or another since the time of Descartes. It is a view backed up by the deep-

---

[3] Ikemi Yūjirō, 池見酉次郎, セルフ・コントロールと禅 *[Zen and Self-Con-trol]* (NHK Books, 1981).

rooted inner desire of people that even if the flesh dies, the spirit will not — an idea in line with traditional religious ideas of the West which see spirit as separate from body. The same way of thinking had circulated in Japan under the name of the Buddha Dharma, but was rigorously rejected by Dōgen. For him, the idea that "spirit is eternally undying and the body alone dies" was not the Buddha Dharma but the false view of unbelief.

According to Professor Ikemi, once when Dōgen's ideas were introduced at an International Conference of Psychosomatic Medicine, the result was such a great interest in Zen — particularly in Dōgen's Zen as the soul of the "Wisdom of the East" — that one of the participants went so far as to exclaim, "Let medicine return to the East!"

THE BUDDHIST IDEA OF "BODY AND MIND AS ONE"

Dōgen's theory of "body and mind as one" appears clearly in the chapter of his *Shōbōgenzō* known as "Discourse on Practice." It is worth our while to reproduce in its entirety an exchange that takes place between Master Dōgen and one of his listeners. First, the question is posed to him:

> Some have said, "Do not grieve over birth-and-death. There is a way to rid yourself of birth-and-death promptly, by knowing the reason for the eternal immutability of the so-called mind-nature. The gist here is that, although once the body is born it is inevitably destined to die, this mind-nature can never perish. If you realize that the mind-nature, which is not subject to birth-and-death, exists in your own body, you make it your fundamental nature. Therefore, the body is its temporary form, and it dies here and lives there, without termination. Yet the mind is forever immutable, unchanging throughout past, present, and future. It is said that to know this is to be free from birth-and-death. Those who know it will put a final end to the birth-and-death hitherto in effect, and when their body dies they enter the ocean of true existence. As they stream into this ocean they are endowed with

wondrous virtue, like that of buddha-tathāgatas. Even if you understand this in your present existence, because your body is composed of the erroneous behavior of your past existence, you are different from the saints. Those who fail to grasp this are ever caught up in birth-and-death. Therefore, one must simply know without delay the significance of the mind-nature's immutability. What can come of spending one's whole life sitting quietly, doing nothing?" Do you think such an idea is truly in accord with the way of the buddhas and patriarchs?

Now let us listen to Dōgen's reply:

> The view you have just expounded is definitely not the Buddha Dharma, but the view of the Senika heresy.
>
> This view holds that in one's body there is a spiritual intelligence. As occasions arise this intelligence readily discriminates likes and dislikes, yes and no; it knows pain and irritation, suffering and pleasure. They all proceed from this spiritual intelligence. However, when the body perishes this spiritual nature separates from the body and is reborn in another place. Therefore, while it seems to perish here, it has life elsewhere, and thus is ever immutable, never perishing. Such is the view of the Senika heresy.
>
> But to learn this view and try to set it up as the Buddha Dharma is more foolish than picking up a roof tile or pebble and supposing it to be a golden jewel. The deplorability of such a foolish illusion is without parallel. Hui-chung of the T'ang dynasty warned strongly against it. Is it not foolish to allow this false view — that the mind abides and the form perishes — to be equated with the wondrous Dharma of the buddhas; while thus producing the fundamental cause of birth-and-death, to think you are freed from birth-and-death? It is to be greatly pitied. Just recognize that it is a false, non-Buddhist view, and do not lend your ear to it.
>
> I am compelled by the nature of the matter, as well as for compassion's sake, to deliver you from your mistaken understanding. You should know that the Buddha Dharma from

the first preaches that body and mind are not two, that substance and form are not two. This is equally known in India and in China, and there can be no doubt about it. Need I mention that in the teaching of immutability, all things are immutable, regardless of the difference between body and mind? In the teaching of perishability, all things are perishable, regardless of the difference of substance and form. In this light, why speak of the body perishing and the mind abiding? Is it not contrary to the right and fundamental principle? Not only that, you must realize that birth-and-death is in and of itself *nirvāṇa*. Buddhism has never spoken of *nirvāṇa* apart from birth-and-death. Indeed, by understanding that the mind, separated from the body, is immutable, you mistakenly estimate that it is the Buddha-wisdom free from birth-and-death. Yet the very mind that makes this discriminatory judgment is still subject to birth-and-death, and is simply not immutable. Is this not futile?

You should give this deep deliberation: the Buddha Dharma has always maintained the oneness of body and mind. Thus, how is it that while your body is born and perishes, the mind alone, separated from the body, is not caught up in birth-and-death? If at one time body and mind were one, and at another time not one, the Buddhist teaching would surely be an empty lie. Moreover, to think that birth-and-death is something to be eliminated is a sin of hating the Buddha Dharma. You must guard against such thinking.

Understand this: the teaching in the Buddha Dharma that the mind-nature is the great and all-embracing characteristic of all phenomena, referring to the universe as a whole, does not make distinctions between form and nature, or speak of difference between birth and annihilation. Even enlightenment and *nirvāṇa* are nothing other than this mind-nature. All dharmas — the myriad forms dense and close of the universe — are simply this one Mind, including all, excluding none. These various dharma-gates are all the same one Mind. To speak of there being no disparity at all between them is the way Buddhists understand the nature of mind.

Thus, in this single Dharma should one be differentiating
body and mind, and dividing birth-and-death and *nirvāṇa*?
We are all originally children of Buddha, so do not listen to
the wagging tongues of madmen relating non-Buddhist
views.[4]

There are plenty of people around who think that since Japan is a
Buddhist country, they can say, "I am a Buddhist," and not a few of
them wrongly suppose that it is Buddhist to believe that "the mind
remains while the body perishes." Clearly Dōgen rejected this as an
erroneous, un-Buddhist understanding of the doctrine of "body and
mind as one." For Buddhism, there is always a "nonduality of form
and substance."

ZEN BUDDHISM AND POST-MODERN AWARENESS

The idea of the body-mind unity is not unique to Dōgen. As the
Master himself says, it is a fundamental idea of Buddhist believers as
a whole, "the way Buddhists understand the nature of mind."

A Buddhist layman once went to visit monk Takusui, one of the
great Zen masters of the Edo period, and said, "The other day I
awakened to the fact that this *body* of mine is finite and will one day
die, but my *mind* is eternal, beyond birth and death. It is like a house
that burns to the ground, while the owner escapes unharmed."

On hearing this Takusui upbraided the man in a loud voice, "This
is the false view of an unbeliever!" Then he told him this story:[5]

Once upon a time Hyōsasen said of the picture of a death-skull,
"The outer shell is here but the man is somewhere else. That is, the
spirit is out of the pouch."

Daie Rōshi observed this and remonstrated, "How can you be
practicing Zen and yet see things so wrongly? The simple shell *is* the
man: spirit-in-pouch, pouch-in-spirit."

---

[4] Cited from the translation of N. Waddell and M. Abe, *The Eastern Buddhist*
4.1 (1971): 145-48.

[5] See 大慧記 [*The Record of Daie*], ed. by Araki Kengo 荒木見悟 (Tokyo:
Chikuma Shobō, 1969).

This is what is meant by "body and mind as one." When we begin to differentiate the *ideas* of body and mind, flesh and spirit, in no time we find ourselves thinking as if the *reality* itself were somehow two. But what actually exists is only the "one body-mind." There is no mind or spirit apart from this outer shell of a body. "Body" and "mind" are distinguishable but inseparable, an original "body and mind as one."

There are limits to the way Western medicine tries to explain the way the body works, first by looking at the human being as a physical composition of natural elements, and then proceeding to dissect it biologically. In contrast, the Eastern way of seeing the human as "spirit-in-pouch, pouch-in-spirit," or "body and mind as one," does not separate body from mind and then look at the fleshly body as an object of natural science. It sees the body of a single body-mind. This is what makes the "Eastern view of the body" so completely different from the "corporeal" view of Western medicine.

This means that I, the doctor, although distinguishable from my patient, am inseparable. "Self and other are not two." This is why "this self" that I am can directly share in the sufferings of the *other self* who is my patient. The essence of "Buddhist medicine" lies in imitating the great doctor-king, Śākyamuni, or at least in trying to be a small doctor-king.

The Buddhist ideas of "body and mind as one" and the "nonduality of self and other" are not as difficult as they sound before we stop to think about them. But what is more important is that doctors begin to practice on their own the threefold learning of Precept, Meditation, and Wisdom — regulating one's lifestyle by vowing to keep the Precepts, entering with one's body-mind well attuned into the harmonious unity of Meditation, and awakening to the Original Self through the experience of *prajñā*. Would this not open the way to a therapy for the actual living human body-mind as such, to a "new medicine"?

I repeat: *If medicine's basic view of the human is in error, what kind of medicine can it be?*

Allow me to state my conclusions as forthrightly as I can. The modern notion of the ego rests on the credo, "In the beginning was the ego." In place of this idea, which I have characterized as a "sickness unto death" for human beings, I would stress a Buddhist, and more deeply human, insight (*prājña*) which reads, "In the beginning was non-ego." This non-ego, or *anātman*, belongs to the philosophy of *śūnyatā* we find in the *Heart Sūtra*. The term *śūnyatā* represents the dialectic of awakening to existence by *transcending* it, of seeking to affirm the self by *denying* the ego. This is the "enlightened wisdom" of *prajñā*. "If there is no ego, all is self." It is an awakening to the Original Fact of human existence—the "nonduality of self and other," the fact that my self and the self of others, that I and things, are distinguishable but inseparable. This idea of awakening to the Original Self—that is, the awakening of the post-modernist who has gone beyond the modernist—seems to me to capture the contemporary philosophical significance of Buddhism.[6]

To illustrate the point I would like to return to the protagonist of Sōseki's novel whom I mentioned earlier. The man, Nagai Daisuke, is a man of about thirty years of age who has awakened to the modern ego. He finds himself in the unadmirable position of having every reason to be happy but suffering from a debilitating *ennui* that is eating away at his spirit from within. His own salvation is when he is in the presence of his lover, Michiyo, who happens to be the wife of a friend of his. He tries to repress his affections for her, but in the end gives up trying to live by "will" and decides to live by "nature." He calls her to him and confesses, "I need you to exist, I absolutely need you."

The words are far more than a simple confession of love by a man for a woman; they point to the awareness of a "new self" that touches the very foundations of humanness, to a "nonduality of self and other," where I and Thou can be distinguished but not separated, where the human being cannot live alone. *I need you to exist.* Persons are able to become a self only when they love another.

---

[6] Concerning my theory of the post-modern age, see 現代を生きる禅 *Living Zen Today]*, vol. 1 of *Collected Writings of Akizuki Ryōmin* (see above, 19, n.7).

A few lines above, I stated, "In the beginning was the no-self." At the end of the last chapter, I paraphrased Buber's view as, "In the beginning was the *relationship*." Taken together, the two represent the Buddhist idea of *śūnyatā* as the "non-duality of self and other." To make the ego truly empty and enter into the realm of no-ego, one invariably lands in the realm of a relationship based on the nonduality of self and other. The disciple of Zen expresses this as a deictic of direct experience in the words, "If there is no ego, all is self." Emptiness means living the dialectic of dying to the ego and living in the Original Self where self and other are nondual. What Buber speaks of as relationship early Buddhism calls *pratītya-samutpāda dharma-dhātu*, the Dharma realm of dependent origination, and in the Mahāyāna tradition it is what Kegon refers to as "all phenomena in the world blending with each other without impediment." Awakening to this new and yet original true person in whom self and other are nondual is nothing other than the *prajñā* wisdom of enlightenment. This is the primary meaning of the Buddha way. The cure for the illness of modern civilization lies in establishing a new human subject, and that is just what *prajñā* enlightenment is.

Reflective individuals in today's world look eagerly to Buddhism as a source of such exceptional wisdom. This is the reason why psychosomatic medicine has turned enthusiastically to Zen. There, too, is where relationships between doctor and patient, nurse and patient, need to be rethought.

I would go further: the entire field of medical science as such needs rethinking.

10　A Buddhist Comment on the "New Science"

"NEW AGE SCIENCE" AND BUDDHISM

In the latter half of the 1960s, a new movement emerged in the scientific world known as "New Age Science." Like psychosomatic medicine, it was centered mainly in the United States. The year before last, at the invitation of a voluntary association of scientists headed by the Crown Prince Mikasa-no-miya, Fritjof Capra, one of the leading figures of this new movement, came to Japan for a stay of about one month. The author of the celebrated books *The Tao of Physics* and *The Turning Point* (both of which have been translated into Japanese), he has been hailed as a forerunner of the "new science." Before Capra's works had become widely known, Yukawa Hideki[1] recommended them to Matsuoka Seigō, director of the Kōsakusha publishing house. Impressed by what he read in *The Tao of Physics*, Matsuoka, with the help of Capra's close friend Yoshifuku Shin'ichi,[2] arranged for the translation and publication of the book. As the Chinese word *Tao* in the title suggests, the approach represents an entirely new scholarly attempt to understand the problems

---

[1] Yukawa Hideki 湯川秀樹 is Professor Emeritus of Kyoto University and a Nobel laureate in physics.

[2] Yoshifuku Shin'ichi 吉福伸逸 , a noted critic of New Age Science, is one of those responsible for introducing the movement to Japan.

at the cutting edge of contemporary physics with the aid of Oriental thought. Thinkers pursuing this approach have inaugurated a movement to reexamine the foundations of science up to the present by comparing "modern European scientific thought" with "Eastern mysticism."

Another link in the process was a widely publicized international conference on "transpersonal psychology" held three years ago in Kyoto. Professor Kawai Hayao of Kyoto University, one of the central figures of the conference, noted frankly that he had had some initial reservations concerning this brand of psychology. The more deeply he went into it, however, the more he felt something new brewing in the world of psychology, and decided to coordinate the international conference himself and co-edit its proceedings.[3] I had received an invitation to this conference as an authority on Zen, but for reasons of health had to decline. From the Buddhist side Nishitani Keiji Sensei and Professor Tamaki Kōshirō were in attendance.

Two years ago, in the fall of 1986, I had a brief meeting with Dr. Capra in Tokyo through the kind help of Yoshifuku and another young friend, Okano Moriya.[4] Another meeting, which was to take place in the summer of 1987 on the occasion of the International Buddhist-Christian Conference in Berkeley, did not materialize because of a conflict of schedules.

On the Japanese side, the activities of this New Age Science have tended to follow a single track, namely, to give greater academic respectability to a "new science" intent on offsetting a one-sided reliance on scientific proof. I refer here to a group centered on Shimizu

---

[3] Kawai Hayao 河合隼雄 is Japan's leading Jungian psychologist. Together with Yoshifuku Shin'ichi, he edited the proceedings of the conference under the title 宇宙意識への接近 [Approaching Cosmic Consciousness] (Tokyo: Shunjūsha, 1987). Kawai touched on some of the issues brought up in the conference in a subsequent book of his own entitled 宗教と科学の接点 Points of Convergence between Science and Religion] (Tokyo: Iwanami, 1986).

[4] Okano Moriya 岡野守也 is an editor of Shunjūsha, a major Japanese publishing house.

Hiroshi, professor of biophysics at Tokyo University. Ever since a meeting he had with the novelist Endō Shūsaku and Yagi Seiichi at a conference on "Overcoming the Modern Ego," he has been called on frequently in this connection. He is joined by Matsuoka Seigō and the philosopher Nakamura Yūjirō. Nakamura is one of the leading representatives in Japan today of French philosophy; Matsuoka is one of the representative critics of contemporary Japan who straddles the fields of science and religion. I myself have had my perspective greatly expanded as a result of these thinkers.[5]

Thus scholars at the very cutting edge of several of the sciences — including, of course, physics, but also biology, medicine, psychology, sociology, and economics — are today rethinking the foundations of several centuries of the discipline known as modern European "science" and groping earnestly to create a "new science." Along with Zen intellectuals in general, followers of the Zen way such as myself have felt a new quickening and begun to draw closer and closer to these thinkers.

Washio Ken'ya,[6] chief editor for arts and sciences at the Kōdansha publishing house and a friend of many years, once remarked to me some years ago, "Scientists around the world today are turning an eager eye in the direction of Eastern thought, and in particular on Zen as its quintessence. But in the world of Japanese Zen, you are about the only one who seems to be responding. Keep it up!" Since that time, and I must say, much to my own dismay, Washio's "prediction" has been fulfilled. People around the world are getting caught up in the vortex of the movement, yet there seems to be no one else thinking about a "Zen living the present." The remainder of this chapter represents my modest attempt to point to that gap, if not to fill it.[7]

---

[5] Shimizu Hiroshi 清水　博, Nakamura Yūjirō　中村雄二郎, Matsuoka Seigō 松岡正剛 .

[6] Washio Ken'ya 鷲尾賢也 .

[7] This chapter consists of a transcript of the first half of a presentation to the Fourth Bioholonics Symposium, to which Akizuki was invited as a panelist by Professor Shimizu. Much of the repetition of material carried in earlier chapters

THE MEANING OF "SENTIENT BEINGS" IN BUDDHISM

After the dark cloud that covered Japan during the years before and after the war had passed, we found ourselves in a bright new era in which philosophy came to life again. It was during these years that I did my philosophical studies at Tokyo University. In no time at all I found myself among the stragglers, but to my good fortune I was taken under wing by Suzuki Daisetz Sensei and began to walk the way of Zen, as I have continued to do to this day. But as the elder statesman of postwar philosophy in Japan, Mutai Risaku Sensei, once told me, "Like it or not, you have tasted the fruit of philosophy." Quite so, and probably this is why I got it into my head to be more than a simple practitioner of Zen — to become a Zen thinker. In that capacity, I would like here to offer some random thoughts regarding what Buddhism has to say to the future of scientific, technological culture. Let us begin by reflecting on how Buddhism understands "living things."

In Buddhism, living things are referred to as "sentient beings," a term that stems finally from the Sanskrit word *sattva*. "Sentient beings" includes everything that has life, but refers in particular to the masses of human beings. Still more particularly, Buddhism understands the term to mean "the strays" among human beings, as opposed to "the awakened" or buddhas.

The comprehensive term *sentient* connotes "to be alive with a sense of life," in contrast to flowers and trees, mountain and rivers, and other "non-sentient" things of earth. If we take *sense* here to mean *conscious sensation*, the distinction is only provisional.[8] The

has been eliminated, as well as remarks specific to the audience that was listening to him.

[8] Japanese uses the Chinese rendering of *sattva*, *shujō* 衆生 , to refer to sentient beings in general, and *shunin* 衆人 for human beings. Literally these terms mean "the mass of living beings" and the "mass of people" respectively. The Chinese translation used for later Buddhist texts is "sentient beings" (有情 , literally, "that which has sensation") in contrast to non-sentient things (非有情 or 無情).

reason is that, seen from the radical standpoint of the Buddha's *satori*, sentient and non-sentient are the same. There is a line in the *Kegon Sūtra* which reads:

> If one Buddha attains enlightenment, when one looks at the whole world of dharmas, the grass and trees, the land, all become Buddha.

As the Zen saying has it:

> Śākyamuni the Buddha looks in *satori* at the morning star and says, "I and the great earth and all sentient beings have attained enlightenment together."[9]

One can also translate this latter phrase as "I and the great earth *of* sentient beings." In other words, that in addition to the simultaneous enlightenment of the sentient beings of the earth and one's own "self," we can also speak of a simultaneous enlightenment of sentient beings, the self, and the earth.

In the same *Kegon Sūtra*, we read:

> All sentient beings have the Tathāgata's power of *prajñā*.

And in the *Nirvāṇa Sūtra* we find the oft-repeated passage:

> All living beings without exception have the Buddha-nature.

In this case, the condition of "becoming Buddha and looking at the whole world of dharmas" is absent and all things are said directly to contain the "Buddha-nature" (the essence of the Buddha, the original purity of mind). The idea of Buddha-nature is often interpreted to mean "the possibility of becoming a Buddha," but this puts becoming a Buddha *in the future*, and hence does not refer to the essence of the Self *in the here-and-now*. And if this were the case, as I

[9] From the *Denkōroku* 伝光録 . See T 82.343-411.

have been saying for a long time, we could not even begin to speak of Zen.

Thus, in the last analysis, Buddhism clearly understands "*sentient beings* as referring to both the sentient and the non-sentient," the animate and the inanimate. What can the term refer to, however, if "living" includes both what is alive with a conscious sense of life and what is alive without it?

When people accustomed to Western modes of thought hear this sort of talk, they all too easily rush to the conclusion that it is some form of hylozoism or animism. In fact, the standpoint from which such a statement is made is completely different. There are also those who see Buddhism as a kind of pantheism, but this is definitely not the case either. Still other scholars speak of a "panbuddhism," but I tend to agree with those who see this as merely another form of pantheistic interpretation.

THE RATIONALE FOR INANIMATE SENTIENT BEINGS

There is a beautiful little book in Dōgen's *Shōbōgenzō* entitled "The Scripture of Mountains and Waters."[10] Its theme is reflected in the phrases "The eastern mountains travel on the waters" and "The green mountains are forever walking." In it, Dōgen says:

> Because the *walking* of mountains must be like the walking of people, don't doubt the *walking* of mountains just because it doesn't look the same as the walking of human beings.
>
> If one doubts the *walking* of the mountains, one doesn't even yet know one's own walking either.

And because he can say,

> The green mountains are not animate, not inanimate; the self is not animate, not inanimate.

[10] 山水経 . Quotations here are taken from the translation of Thomas Cleary in *Shōbōgenzō: Zen Essays by Dōgen*. (Honolulu: University of Hawaii Press, 1986), 89-99.

he is also able to offer the sympathetic teaching,

> The *walking* of the *green mountains* as well as the walking
> of oneself should be clearly examined.

Now what can the *subject* of the walking be if it is neither sentient
nor non-sentient? Dōgen replies:

> Just because they are not rationally understood by you,
> that doesn't mean you shouldn't study the road of rational
> understanding of the buddhas and Zen adepts.
> Apart from the path of understanding of the *ignorant*,
> there is the path of understanding of *buddhas and patriarchs*.

Now what can the logic of this "path of understanding of the buddhas and patriarchs" be that has cut off the deliberations of the ignorant, the logic that Buddhism calls "wondrous"? Dōgen refers to it
as "emptiness before signs" and speaks of "the self before the emergence of signs."[11] But what can this mean? If I may begin by stating
my conclusion as baldly as possible, I would say it refers to the *conversion of the subject* who sees. The subject who sees things clearly
converts from an ignorant fool (a sentient being) to one who is enlightened (a Buddha).

Buddhism refers to "one water, four ways of seeing."[12] The human
being sees *water*, the hungry ghost sees *pus and blood*, the fish sees a
place to live, and the angel sees *a place studded with all kinds of jewels*.
In other words, one and the same object appears differently to different subjects.

As we have seen in earlier chapters, Śākyamuni set out in search
of liberation from the suffering of endless transmigration, a liberation to a realm of eternal tranquility and extinction—*nirvāṇa*. While
engaged in the practice of yoga on the quest for *nirvāṇa*, he unexpectedly attained *bodhi* and was enlightened. In the deep realms of

---

[11] See Cleary, *Shōbōgenzō: Zen Essays by Dōgen*, 87.
[12] A common analogy used in the Vijñaptimātratā tradition: the reality of
"water" depends on who is viewing it.

yogic *samādhi* where body and mind are at one, the *ego* became *empty* and his eyes were opened to the "ego of no-ego" (the "true person of no rank" or "Formless Self"). The subject transcended from the ego of the wheel of *saṃsāra* to the Original Self of "neither death nor life, neither unclean nor clean, neither increase nor decrease."[13] This is what I mean by the conversion of the subject.

What is seen in this conversion is "true suchness." The "true person" (Buddha) sees "true suchness" (reality as it truly is). Here the person and the suchness (in Sanskrit, *tathatā* or the "as-it-is-ness" of things) are one. This is what Buddhism circumscribes by terms like *śūnyatā*, "the non-duality of self and other," the "oneness of things and self."

Buddhism always looks at things from the point of view of Buddha as subject, so that seeing never takes leave of the concrete self in the here-and-now. This is precisely why what the ignorant distinguish as "sentient" or "non-sentient" all belong to the same class of "living beings." Living beings and the self are distinguishable but not separable. I live, therefore all is alive — this is the nonduality of things and the self, of self and other.

Such an approach should not be confused with a simple transition from objectivism to subjectivism. It is a conversion occurring at a standpoint prior to the bifurcation of subject and object. What I refer to as the "undivided subject-object" does not mean "what has not yet been divided" but "previously undivided".[14] It is here that the conversion of the subject takes place.

FROM THE BUDDHA'S ENLIGHTENMENT TO A NEW SCHOLARSHIP

The *bodhi* of Śākyamuni may be described as a conversion from the samsaric ego to the nirvanic self. It was a transcendence and self-

---

[13] The phrase is from the *Heart Sūtra*.

[14] This idea of a standpoint prior to the bifurcation of subject and object refers to the pivotal notion in Nishida's *An Inquiry into the Good*. See above, 30, n. 5.

awakening of existential reality. I see a new notion of scholarly inquiry emerging here.

From the time of the Greeks up to the present, scholarly inquiry has consisted of the study of *theoria*. For Aristotle the goal was the *pure form* attained by way of an inner intuition into what was not the object of perceptual knowledge. On this basis he viewed the human as participating in the activity of God, whose essence is *pure thought*. This was the source of the "modern science" of the West. To begin with, science *differentiates* the subjective and objective points of view, attempting as far as possible to bracket subjectivity and to make objectivity the *subject matter*. It further analyzes the objective subject matter into its elements. This, too, is a *differentiation*. It then seeks out the "laws" at work among elements. Once the laws are discovered, they can be adopted to restructure nature and society. This is *techne*. In this way Western civilization has conquered the world of nature through the power of science and technology and forcefully subjugated human beings.

One of the signs of this "force" has been that repulsive modern Western colonial control of "bloodthirsty Christians drowning the voices of people of other faiths who lack the power to control their flocks."[15] The strong critique against "Western modernity" has been the spearhead of the ardent demand for the "post-modern."

Before rushing too far ahead into a critique of modernity, a word of gratitude is in order for the magnificent contributions that "modernity" has made to the human race. In some sense, modernization has been, and at present still is, an important and necessary orientation for human history. In spite of this, the critique of modernity and the call for a turn to the post-modern is a pressing task for today's world. Humanity has already clearly realized that progress in material culture has gone too far ahead of progress in spiritual culture. They see the unhappiness that results from tearing mind away from matter. People shudder at the thought that one slip in the science

---

[15] Attributed by Akizuki to Ueda Bin 上田 敏, a French and English literary critic and poet in his own right.

and technology that is supposed to promote happiness and we end up destroying planet earth itself.

And that is not all. This modern world of ours has brought the very science which gave birth to the core of modern civilization to the state of having to rethink the nature of its own scholarly inquiry from the ground up. This is evident not only to those in the world of philosophy and religion, but all the more so to scientists and technologists.

In its single-minded devotion to a purely objective quest, physics has found itself impelled by the simple idea that without "light" nothing can be perceived, to begin harboring profound doubts about the fundamental notions of science up to the present. Can we simply nod our heads in agreement to the idea that psychology, by effectively restricting itself to the objective subject matter of the *seen* mind, has been unable to arrive at the *seeing* mind which is the mind's original essence?[16] Furthermore, as I explained in the last chapter, psychosomatic medicine has made medical science reflect seriously on the image it has heretofore had of the body as *flesh* or *matter*. In short, the creation of a "new science" is an urgent task for today. It demands a radical reexamination of the foundations of scholarly inquiry.

What are we to say about all of this from the standpoint of religious studies and Buddhist studies? Earlier I touched on the pros and cons of the idea of scholarship championed by the celebrated Tokyo University Buddhist scholar, Ui Hakuju. Ui Sensei did not hesitate to proclaim, "I myself have the faith of the Sōtō sect" — a faith, I would add, that in my own way I also share. But he went on strongly to admonish *against* introducing that faith into the world of scholarly inquiry. "Faith is faith and scholarship is scholarship." If that is forgotten, scholarship is corrupted. This means that Buddhist studies is biased in the direction of history and literature. Thus the tendency comes about to despise the slightly gloomy pronouncements of philosophy. Tamaki Kōshirō was the only one to sound this note in

---

[16] Here again Akizuki is clearly alluding to an idea of Nishida's.

Buddhist studies at Tokyo University. The main point is that what we end up with is a Buddhist studies bereft of the soul of the Buddha.

Something similar has taken place in Christianity, as for instance in the case of Sekine Masao Sensei.[17] His idea of Christian studies is also one in which "faith is faith and scholarship is scholarship," thus fitting hand-in-glove with the idea of Ui Sensei. While I cannot but respect the scholarship of such thinkers, it seems to me that they remain hamstrung by the culture shock of the Meiji period, brought about by the importation of modern Western science.

It is high time for Buddhist studies to give some thought to the creative formation of the "new science" and "scholarly inquiry" that has broken free of the captivity of the modern West. The late Masuda Hideo, a personal friend and fellow traveler on the Buddhist path, has spoken of the need for a "quest-ology."[18] This is why I like to distinguish between the "Zen way" and "Zen studies," two terms which up to the Meiji period were used synonymously. Is there not perhaps a hint here for how to go about rethinking today's idea of scholarly inquiry? The Oriental idea of scholarship as "not yet divided," needs to be taken up again in the face of the "*already* divided," since Buddhist studies must assume the traditional form of the "threefold learning" of Precept, Meditation, and Wisdom.

The scholar of religion Kishimoto Hideo Sensei[19] has taken it as his vocation to root religious studies in Japanese academia *as a science.* I recall once how, after Mutai Sensei had delivered a lecture at the invitation of the Japanese Association for Religious Studies, he told me, "The association is a strange one, isn't it? Scientists of religion and philosophers of religion come together to fight over one issue after another." There are pros and cons to Kishimoto Sensei's

---

[17] Sekine Masao 関根正雄 was a noted Japanese Old Testament scholar.

[18] See Masuda Hideo 増田英男 , 仏教思想 の 求道的研究 [*A Questological Approach to Buddhist Thought*], 2 vols. (Tokyo: Sōbunsha, 1966, 1987).

[19] Kishimoto Hideo 岸本英雄 is Professor Emeritus of Religious Studies at Tokyo University.

approach as well. He himself had studied Indian mysticism and, as an undergraduate and graduate student, practiced Zen meditation under Shaku Jōkō Rōshi together with my strict teacher Osaka Kōryū Rōkan. But for better or for worse, his religious studies never stepped away from the standpoint of modern science.

Although a graduate of Tokyo University, I did not remain within the tradition of Ui Hakuju, but found myself drawn strongly by the Kyoto tradition of Nishida Kitarō Sensei in religious studies, Buddhist studies, and philosophy. To put it frankly, I was not terribly fond of his successor, Tanabe Hajime.[20] His thought, which began with philosophy of science, passed through Dōgen and Shinran to Christianity and Marxism, covering the range of contemporary philosophy. His achievements are admirable enough, but the important notion of "absolute nothingness" that formed the basis was, for Tanabe Sensei, merely a *conceptual requirement*, as he himself clearly stated. What is more, he lacked Nishida Sensei's experiential insight into the notion of "absolute nothingness." At the same time, I find much more affinity with the thought of Tanabe's successor, Nishitani Keiji, under whom I also studied.

Be that as it may, I am convinced that if one sees the *subject* who is doing the scholarly inquiry as a Zen follower directly tied to the *satori* of Śākyamuni, a new idea of scholarship and a new science must needs emerge. In this sense, I have great hopes for the new efforts being made by those working in the field of science itself. What distinguishes my approach from theirs, however, has to do with the matter of *scientific* proof. Let me explain further.

THE HOPES AND CONCERNS OF THE NEW SCIENCE

In the previous chapter I spoke of my interests in psychosomatic medicine and voiced my misgivings about the lack of a proper under-

---

[20] A prominent disciple of Nishida Kitarō. See Tanabe Hajime, *Philosophy as Metanoetics* (Berkeley: University of California Press) and T. Unno and J. Heisig, ed., *The Religious Philosophy of Tanabe Hajime: The Metanoetical Imperative* (Berkeley: Asian Humanities Press, 1990).

standing of the mind-body totality. Similarly, despite my interest in the New Age Science movement, there is something there that still bothers me. A concrete example may help to make the point.

In the course of the 1987 conference on transpersonal psychology referred to at the outset, the transpersonal theoretician, Ken Wilbur, was introduced as "someone who has practiced Rinzai and Sōtō Zen," but according to his *zazen* "master" (if one can use the term) and my fellow disciple of the way, Maezumi Hakuyū Rōshi,[21] he was not what one could call a serious practicer. This seems to me typical of those in the new science movement who take Eastern thought as an "Oriental mysticism" to oppose to "modern Western science." I find the approach misguided.

To begin with, the idea of an East-West polarity is in error. When Suzuki Daisetz Sensei was teaching and writing, this may have still been more or less acceptable, given that the "East" had not yet gained citizenship in the international intellectual forum. Suzuki's efforts to transmit the East to the West, with Buddhism as its quintessential representative and Zen at the center, were pioneering. At the time, the idea that "East is East and West is West" was dominant. There was simply no other model in terms of which to think. But today things have changed. The East can no longer simply be defined as a counterpoint to the West. It must understand itself as the *East of the post-modern world*. To speak of the "East" today is to speak of the world of "the present." The shift of perspective is extremely important.

Even if one restricts one's sights to the world outside of Japan, those in the forefront have no recourse but to make the *about-face* they seem to dread — away from the clumsy insistence on an East-West polarity. For me, this is one of the most important admonitions that need to be voiced today. This needs further thinking out, but I have a sense that the process is already well on its way.

My second concern is that the people of the New Age Science

---

[21] Maezumi Hakuyū 前角博雄 was then director of the Los Angeles Zen Center.

take the East as a single entity and then set up an "Eastern mysticism" in contrast to "modern Western scientific thought." There are two difficulties here. The "Orient," after all, includes India and China, Indochina and Tibet. In China there is Confucian thought, Taoism, and Buddhism. In India there is Hinduism, Buddhism, and Islam. To lump them all together can only invite confusion.

In all of this, what I fear most is an approach that puts Hinduism and Buddhism in the same framework. We may say that Indian religion (Brahmanism and Hinduism) takes as its highest concept the idea from the *Upaniṣads* that "Self and Brahman are one." But Buddhism rejects this identity of Self and Brahman. Rennyo, for example, insists that "Buddhism begins with the non-ego"[22] and maintains his insistence on *anātman* in adamant opposition to any idea of a "Great Self." This is most important and merits careful discussion. It is a problem that will have to be taken up by and by.

Is there any point to placing Buddhism in the realms of "mystical thought"? In middle age, Suzuki Daisetz Sensei spoke clearly of "Zen and mysticism," having seen a profound unity of thought and experience between Zen and Meister Eckhart in his own researches, and finding a clear development of the idea in the work of Nishitani Keiji Sensei and his close friend and colleague, Ueda Shizuteru.[23] But in his late years, Daisetz Sensei in fact became disenchanted with references to Zen as a "mysticism."[24] This is also a topic that calls for further discussion.

---

[22] An outline of the life and thought of this important Pure Land Buddhist figure can be found in Minor and Ann Rogers, *Rennyo*: (Berkeley: Asian Humanities Press, forthcoming).

[23] Ueda Shizuteru 上田閑照 , recently retired from the chair of Philosophy and Religion at Kyoto University, has been laboring on the borderlands between Zen and the mysticism of Meister Eckhart since the time of his doctoral dissertation, *Die Gottesgeburt in der Seele und der Durchbruch zur Gottheit* (Gütersloh: Gerd Mohn, 1965).

[24] See, for example, Suzuki's review of Heinrich Dumoulin's *A History of Zen Buddhism* in *The Eastern Buddhist* 1.1 (1965): 123-26 in which he clearly repudiates his earlier idea of seeing Zen as a form of mysticism. Dumoulin himself has omitted the comparison from his new and greatly expanded two-volume edition.

Such are the reservations I feel amidst my great and profound hopes for the New Age Science movement. My young friends tell me that to say these things just at the time when people of the world have earnestly begun to turn to the East is to douse the fires of their enthusiasm with cold water. But I cannot help myself. The fact is, I want the East, and *Mahāyāna* Buddhism, to be understood correctly, and this is something I want to say above all to those in quest of a "new science." Modern Western science came about by excluding the scientists, the subjects who do the science, from the world of science, as if they were no more than the "eye that looks at the world." From the very outset, subject and object are separated. By bracketing the subjective point of view as much as possible, they hope to look at things objectively. By making everything into an objective subject matter, analyzing it into its components, and eliciting the mechanisms at work among those elements, they come to "laws." And using those laws, we have the "technology" that restructures nature, human beings, and society. However immediately impressive the results of this kind of modern science, this "eye of science" is most assuredly not the "eye of existential humanity." Indeed, the underlying idea of the "modern ego" is itself a "sickness unto death." People have begun to wake up to the fact, which is why they are turning to "the Wisdom of the East" in search of a true view of what it means to be human. We do not stand outside of the world to look at the world. We view it always from within. If, as I am saying, the "subject of science" needs to be re-examined, then it is my further hope that Zen as a way of absolute subjectivity may be a beacon for all in the quest.

11 A Christian's Zen Experience

Permit me to recount one Christian's experience of profound interest for Buddhists.

One of the leading Christians of Japan today is the scholar Yagi Seiichi. His father being one of the close disciples of Uchimura Kanzō,[1] from his early years Yagi was raised in a family of the No-Church Movement, and in his youth experienced a coming to awareness in the faith.

As a graduate student at Tokyo University he spent a period of study abroad in Germany. At the time, the level of understanding of things Japanese was extremely low in Germany and he found himself continually being asked things like, "Do you have automobiles in Japan?" "How many meals a day do the Japanese take?" If he would reply to the last question, "Three," he would be told, "Well what do you know, the same as us!" Subjected to this kind of ridiculous, childish exchange, Yagi prepared about a hundred well-chosen slides and showed them to Germans whenever the occasion presented itself. Naturally, pictures of temples, statues of the Buddha, and Zen gardens were among the slides, which would invariably prompt the question, "What kind of a religion is Buddhism?" To his

---

[1] Uchimura Kanzō 内村鑑三 was a Christian pastor and founder of the No-Church movement in Japan.

embarrassment, Yagi found that, even though he had attended lectures on the intellectual history of the Orient and had read several books on Buddhism, he was unable to give a reply. Again and again he was faced with his own ignorance of things Buddhist. As a scholar from Japan, which is a Buddhist country, devoting himself to the study of Christianity, this was the first time he realized how little he knew about Buddhism.

With that, Yagi borrowed a number of books on Buddhism from a fellow foreign student from Japan. At the time he felt closer to Zen than to Shin Buddhism. Despite the numerous similarities between the figure of Shinran in today's True Pure Land Buddhism and Christianity, for one who confesses Jesus as the "Christ," the idea of converting to a Buddha like Amida Buddha of the Shin tradition, someone who was not the Christ, was unthinkable. At the same time, he felt no resistance in going into Zen Buddhism, which was utterly different from Christianity. Among the several books he read at the time was a book by Suzuki Daisetz Sensei on *No-Mind*.[2] In that book, Daisetz writes, "Put in Christian terms, 'no-mind' means 'Thy will be done.' " These kinds of statements were not unintelligible from a Christian standpoint, but the Zen *mondō* (exchanges between master and disciple) had him completely stymied. In the end he had not the slightest idea what Zen was trying to say.

In this state of mind Yagi went to call on Professor Wilhelm Gundert, who had gone to Japan as a missionary and taught at university and secondary school. He remembered hearing that the man might be a cousin of Hermann Hesse, who had written the celebrated novel on the life of the Buddha, *Siddhartha*. While in Japan, Professor Gundert had had contact with the No-Church of Uchimura Kanzō and become acquainted with Yagi's father, who asked his son to be sure to pay the professor a visit when he was in Germany.

Professor Gundert had come to foster a deep interest in Buddhism from his experience in Japan. Upon returning to his native Ger-

---

[2] 無心ということ (Tokyo: Heibonsha, 1961).

many, he assumed a post as professor in Hamburg University's Department of Japanese Studies and later went on to become president of the university. After retirement, he moved to a house in the picturesque southern German town of Ulm on the banks of the Danube, where he devoted himself to a German translation of the *Hekiganroku*.[3] Eventually he was to complete his translation of this important treasure of Japanese and Chinese Zen dating from the twelfth century, a work which has been called "the primary text of the sect," but when Yagi and another friend from Japan visited him in August of 1951, he was still in the midst of his labors.

It may have been on that first visit, or perhaps on a later one, that the old professor saw Yagi off to the station and presented him with an offprint of the translation of the first part of the *Hekiganroku*. Yagi himself thinks that it may have had something to do with the fact that the first time his father and Professor Gundert had met in Japan, the latter had talked incessantly of Bodhidharma.

The offprint presented the original Chinese with its corresponding German translation on facing pages and included a commentary by Professor Gundert. After his traveling companion left the train at Mainz, Yagi boarded an express train for the return trip from Ulm to Göttingen. During the four-hour ride he read through the German translation of the *Hekiganroku*. Having read books on Zen by Suzuki with the feeling that he half understood what Zen was about, Yagi threw himself into the work reflectively.

> Emperor Wu of Liang asked Bodhidharma, "What is the first principle of the holy teachings?" Bodhidharma said, "Wide open, nothing holy."[4]

---

[3] The translation was published as *Bi-yän-lu: Meister Yüan-wu's Niederschrift von der Smaragdenen Felswand* (Munich: Carl Hanser, 1960-1973), 3 vols. English translations of the work have been done by T. and J. C. Cleary (Boulder, Col.: Shambala, 1977), 3 vols. and by K. Sekida in *Two Zen Classics: Mumonkan and Hekiganroku* (Tokyo: Weatherhill, 1977).

[4] Yagi used the German here. The translation into English has had to be adjusted to fit Gundert's rendition. See *Two Zen Classics*, 147.

He found it easy to read pensively as he was sitting alone in a four-seat section of the train. When he could not make sense of the Chinese he would turn to the German and vice-versa; and when he couldn't make sense of either, he would set the book aside and think. As he wrestled with the text, time passed quickly but left him exhausted.

As he looked up, the train was just passing through Kassel. He stared out the window and watched absentmindedly as the rugged terrain sped by with its forest and fields. The rain had lifted and the clouds were moving aside to make room for the bright blue sky. His mind turned from its intense concentration on the problem of the "Wide open, nothing holy" and emptied itself in the clear sky above. All of a sudden the words returned to his mind's eye in a flash, "Wide open, nothing holy." Without thinking he exclaimed aloud, "Aha!" and jumped up from his seat. Sure enough, nothing had changed. Everything in the surroundings outside the window was exactly as it was before, and yet . . . it had become absolutely new. Things were different from what they were when he was staring absentmindedly a short while before. It was as if a shackles fixed about his head had suddenly split apart and fallen away. He calmed himself and fell back in his seat again, looking about on all sides. What happened, he asked himself, but could not answer.

The first words that came to his mind were these: "Up until now, I had always thought a tree was a tree. *Where did I go wrong?*"

Yagi first spoke of this experience in the train at Kassel several decades later in a "Zen-Christian Discussion" held in eastern Japan to which he had been invited by friends from the United States. In attendance were the young Buddhist scholars Nara Yasuaki[5] of the

---

[5] Nara Yasuaki 奈良康明 , Professor at Komazawa University and one of Japan's leading Indologists, is a Sōtō monk and a leading disciple of Nakamura Hajime.

[6] Nishimura Eshin 西村恵信 is Professor of Religion in Hanazono University's Department of Buddhist Studies. A Rinzai monk and leading figure in Japan's Buddhist-Christian dialogue, Nishimura published a Japanese translation of H. Dumoulin's *Christianity Meets Buddhism* (La Salle: Open Court, 1974).

Sōtō sect and Nishimura Eshin[6] of the Rinzai sect, and Yagi from the Christian side. Among the senior members in attendance were Zen Masters Yamada Reirin, Chancellor of Komazawa University who was later to become the chief abbot of Eihei-ji, Yamada Mumon, President of Hanazono University who would later take over the leadership of Myōshin-ji, and the Chief Abbot of Nanzen-ji, Shibayama Zenkei. Mumon Rōshi responded to Yagi's account by relating his own experience of awakening. He concluded, acknowledging Yagi's experience, "This is not something peculiar to me — Yagi said the same thing. It is an experience that touches the very foundations of religion."

After his experience in the train through Kassel, Yagi quickly came to an understanding of Buddhist thought and grew progressively close to Buddhism, leading him to publish an important book, *Points of Convergence between Christianity and Buddhism*.[7] Later I was to meet Yagi through participating in these meetings and we would come to co-author a number of books.[8]

ZEN EXPERIENCE, ZEN CONSCIOUSNESS, ZEN THOUGHT

What is "Zen experience"? Nothing more than the vigorous forcing aside of intellectual understanding. As the Zen saying has it, "Hot and cold are things you *know*." This is precisely why it makes no sense at all to people in society at large who are straying about aimlessly. To understand the Buddhist realm of enlightenment, one must oneself *become* Buddha. This is what is meant by Dōgen's insistence that "only a Buddha communicates with a Buddha." Just as it is not through *talking about* hot and cold but only by *taking a drink* that one can say one *knows* the difference between hot and cold, so, too, enlightenment or *satori* is a matter of experience. As long as one has not experienced it intimately for oneself but only thought about

---

[7] キリスト教と仏教の接点 (Kyoto: Hōzōkan, 1975).

[8] Their jointly authored works include 禅とイエス・キリスト [*Zen and Jesus Christ*] (Tokyo: Seidosha, 1989); 親鸞とパウロ [*Shinran and St. Paul*] (Tokyo: Seidosha, 1989).

it intellectually and toyed with the words, one is no more than a "scholar" drawing inferences and writing them up in books. In the phrase of Dōgen, such a one is a "teacher-monk."[9] The scholar, of course, begins by not knowing anything at all, and only after diligent reading of the literature, comes to get a picture of the subject matter. Since scholars are generally people with a pretty good head on their shoulders, it stands to reason that they should be able to make some sense of things by reading the literature. And then, applying their own powers of discrimination, they write it up. But religious persons begin with experience. The problem is that they often lack the power of expression or discursive thinking to write down what happens to them, or at least to write it down eloquently. This leads to the peculiar result that the books of clear-thinking scholars, who have had no experience of their own, sell.

"Religious experience" can only occur in the realm of "consciousness." It is completely closed off to the world of dogs and cats. Zen *experience* is always Zen *consciousness*. If it were only a matter of knowing hot and cold by experience, the dogs and cats would manage it without much difficulty. But human experience, including the experience of Zen, engages consciousness. And once consciousness has been engaged it develops to the point of intellectual expression. This is why we must speak not only of Zen consciousness but also of Zen *thought*. Daisetz Sensei's notion of "the history of Zen thought" extends this process to include historical development.

Moreover, as an experience becomes conscious and takes shape as Zen thought, the disposition, upbringing, education that one brings to an experience figure in as important elements. Thus the very same experience of its own leads to different intellectual expressions. Just as the Zen of Master Dōgen, Master Bankei, and of Master Hakuin are all three *Japanese* Zen and yet all three distinct, the "Zen experience" they share in some sense leads to versions of "Zen thought" that seem to head in opposite directions.

---

[9] The translators were not able to locate in Dōgen's texts the term Akizuki uses here, 教者法師 .

"I HAVE SEEN TRUE SUCHNESS" — YAGI'S OWN EXPLANATION

The experience in the train in Kassel which Mumon Rōshi acknowledged as touching the very foundations of religion, did not make very much sense at first for Yagi himself. But once he had regained his composure, he was able to find the words to express it *consciously*, and with time to explain it *intellectually*.

The first impression to reach consciousness and be verbalized, Yagi said, was: "Up until now, I had always thought a tree is a tree [probably due to the fact that he was looking out the window and the first thing that struck his eye were the trees]. Where did I go wrong?" When he later tried to expand on this, he came to the following explanation, clearly at the level of *thought*. I quote him at length:

> Take a plum tree for example. When we say, "This plum tree is a plum tree," we take the subject of the statement to be a real plum tree and the predicate refers to the general concept of a plum tree. The first term, "this plum tree," is a single, concrete reality, but the appended words "is a plum tree" refers to a social convention, an abstract concept. This constitutes the predicate. For instance, peach trees and apricot-almond trees belong to the same genus of "plum tree." In the spring they burst into the same bright, splendid red and white blossoms; their fruits can be pickled and dried or made into plum wine. Everyone knows this and so it belongs to the conceptual content of what a plum tree is. This is the predicate, and it belongs to the general sentence expressed in the form, "S is P." The predicate P represents the socially conventional notion in which the subject S is embraced. As a result of connotation and dissolution, P in fact has come to take predominance over S. When we say, "This plum tree is a plum tree," the plum tree in the predicate, since it is a social convention, does not include the real plum tree in its "true suchness." Once something has been given a connota-

tion this way and dissolved into social convention, social convention takes precedence.

As human beings we are born into a world of "words." Unlike Adam and Eve in the biblical story, we do not first come into contact with "entities" around us and only then give them "names." We begin by learning the "words," then pick up their conceptual content, and finally know individual things like plum trees which are embraced in this conceptual content. Things were different for Adam, it would appear. As the first human being, whenever he came in touch with an "entity" *for the very first time,* he gave it a "name." This is probably what Buddhism means by "true suchness." Not so for us, who are born into a world of words, hear them spoken, learn what they mean from our mother and father, and then know things like particular plum trees as things contained in the concept. As a result, the social convention P takes precedence over the individual entity S. In the example of the plum tree, we first learn about plum trees from our parents and only afterwards know a particular thing to be the sort of plum tree we have been taught about. In this way we are supposed to understand plum trees. But is this really the way to understand a concrete plum tree?

In this way, "conceptuality," which is not equivalent to reality, decides the being of an "entity." Consequently the true entity — its so-called true suchness — eludes our view. Plum trees are one thing, but what about fellow human beings? The Germans have one set of conventions about the Japanese. Then a Japanese shows up, and they think in terms of their conventions. Since the social conventions take precedence, they presume that the individual in front of them corresponds to their notion. And on that basis, as an individual who fits the mold of their conventions, they expect him to behave accordingly and even require it. If the average level of understanding happens to be low, the results can be peculiar in the extreme. Lacking firsthand contact with actual reality, their social conventions determine what reality should look like in advance. And if the one who has suffered this determination should object to the stupidity of it all, he will only find himself alienated from the world of personal intercourse. All "interpersonal communication" collapses. When *social convention* takes precedence over *existence*, there is no avoiding distortion. Thus the existential reality of the "original self" of human beings is not something to be grasped and determined by way of pre-conceptions. This was the first time I had reflected on what it means to understand "reality" from given "ideas."

What my eyes were opened to was the immense error of trying to understand things by beginning with something like a social convention. In the case of Christianity, too, in understanding things by beginning from the scriptures, the words of the scriptures take precedence over the facts. On the grounds that "The bible says so," one looks at the world in a determined way. One must rather see clearly what it means to take the ineluctable existential "fact" of "human existence" as prior to "words." Heretofore the concept has taken precedence over the reality and then turned around to determine what reality is. Is this not a topsy-turvy illusion? Is not the idea that words are prior to things precisely what the *Heart Sūtra* means when it talks of "thought-coverings."[10]

[10] The Sanskrit compound behind the English expression refers to impediments that block one from perceiving things as they truly are. The Chinese translation 顛倒夢想 , which Yagi uses, would translate literally as "topsy-turvy dream-idea."

The passage cited here is from Yagi's キリスト教は信じうるか *[Can Christianity be Believed?]* (Tokyo: Kōdansha Gendai Shinsho No. 243, 1970).

12 Christian-Buddhist Dialogue

MUMON RŌSHI'S RELIGIOUS EXPERIENCE

When he was a student at Tōyō University, Yamada Mumon Rōshi practiced Zen under Kawaguchi Ekai,[1] known as the first to have transmitted Tibetan esoteric Buddhism to Japan. Since Mumon's elder brother had died of tuberculosis, it looked as if the household in which he was raised had been infected,[2] and indeed he himself contracted the disease. In his case, however, it was a result of nutritional deficiency stemming from the rigors of temple life. After rising early each morning to do the cleaning and make preparations for the meal, he would go to university and return late in the day, only to face more household chores and a night of study. Kawaguchi Ekai Rōshi's mother would take the young Mumon aside from time to time and press some money in his hand. "Here, Chōyan (Mumon Rōshi's nickname), use this to buy some fish to cook and eat, but don't tell my son about it." Ekai Rōshi kept the *vinaya* of the Tibetan esoteric tradition strictly, but the young disciple could not help thinking to himself, "The pure monk is lacking in filial piety."

In any case, the severities led to a serious case of tuberculosis and

---

[1] Kawaguchi Ekai 川口慧海 taught at Taishō University and was one of the pioneers in the study of Tibetan Buddhism in Japan. His work *Three Years in Tibet* was translated into English in 1909 (Madras: Theosophist Office).

[2] It was believed that tuberculosis was hereditary at the time. This meant that if one member of the family were to die of the disease, the household would be presumed infected, making it difficult, for example, for other members to marry.

he had to be hospitalized. After the doctors had done all they could, he left the hospital and went to "convalesce at home." At the time, as everyone knew, this meant waiting to die.

One day he was sitting at home, perhaps outside on the porch overlooking the garden. A cool wind crossed his fevered cheeks and he thought to himself:

> What is this thing we call the wind? Of course, wind is air. And if that's so, then it was the air that just passed . . . Even though I haven't paid any attention to it, the air had been there with me from the moment I was born, giving me life.

Without air, humans die. This vital element had been there all along, silently giving life. And not only the air, but sun and water and food as well. Then it struck him: "Here I thought I was living by myself, but actually I was living only because I was being kept alive." This was the first time that Mumon Rōshi awakened to the world of religion. He had realized the existence of the "individual" and the "transindividual."

There is an autobiographical novel by Kurata Hyakuzō entitled *A Co-radiant Life.*[3] Compared with his earlier play, *The Homeless Monk and his Disciples*, which Romain Rolland has praised as the greatest twentieth century work of religious literature, the work may not be great literature, but I would like to cite something from near the beginning of the book:

> If you want to know what it means not to be able to live on your own power, not to have the strength to stay alive by yourself, all you have to do is look at a baby.

If a baby is left entirely on its own at birth, it is certain to die of cold and starvation. Only if its parents are there to raise it, and if not them, then someone else to take their place, can a child survive. So,

---

[3] 光り会ういのち (Tokyo: Shinseisha, 1940). Kurata Hyakuzō 倉田百三 was a playwright and distinguished authority on modern religious literature.

too, the idea that someone can survive without food and water and air, completely "on their own," is out of the question.

Zen is often said to be a religion for oneself alone, and I have to agree. But it is wrong to conclude that Zen is therefore a religion of "self-power."[4] As long as religion is religion, it must not be a religion of self-power. There is simply no such thing as living on one's own.

Mumon Rōshi, on coming to the realization that he had not been *living* but rather had been *being kept alive*, composed the following short verse:

> Something great there is that gives me life,
> The chill of the morning wind has taught me.

This was his first religious experience.

Later Mumon Rōshi was cured of his tuberculosis by a Zen monk who applied the "loquat-leaf cure," and once freed of the malady enrolled as a student at the Hanazono University in Kyoto. On his own account, he wavered back and forth in his heart between Christianity and Buddhism. Sometimes, though wearing the robes of a young Buddhist novice, he would even go to church on Sunday. So great was his devotion, that it seems he was even permitted to preach in the pastor's place!

MUMON RŌSHI'S ZEN EXPERIENCE

In keeping with the Rinzai tradition to which it belongs, Hanazono University sets aside periods from time to time for Zen *sesshin*, which consists of living for a week in a monastery and practicing *zazen*. The temple of Enpuku-ji, located in a place outside Kyoto called Yahata, is used for this purpose. Practice in the Rinzai sect involves not only *zazen* but also the practice of the kōan. Having received a kōan from one's spiritual director, one enters the room of the *rōshi* for a question-and-answer form of "Dharma-debate."

---

[4] The followers of Pure Land Buddhism characterize their own faith as depending on "Other-power" (他力) and other schools, especially Zen, as depending on one's own "self-power" (自力).

This form of discipleship is called "solitary visit" or "entering the room." If the disciple's answer is found wanting, the *rōshi* sounds a small hand bell. This signals the end of the interview. The disciple retires from the *rōshi's* room to the Zen hall where he returns to *zazen* to ponder again a response to the kōan he has received. Sitting in meditation "concentrated and undisturbed," the disciple devises a new response to the kōan and returns to the *rōshi's* room to report. Most of the time the response is flatly rejected by a tinkle of the bell and the disciple must return once again to *zazen*.

Young Mumon, still suffering from his malady, was sitting in meditation. Directly across from him a student was seated solemnly in the posture of meditation. Seeing this, the young Mumon felt his competitive nature rise and, not to be outdone, put all his energy into meditating. When it was time for a recess, everyone got up from meditation to stretch their legs and move about, but the dignified figure seated in front of him did not budge. He remained there, motionless, throughout the recess. This young man would later go on to become Shirōzu Rōshi, master of the Heirin-ji Zen hall. Prior to entering Hanazono, he had practiced at a Zen temple in Kyūshū. In any event, with the help of this school friend, the young Mumon was able to make great progress in Zen, and never tired of stressing what a blessing it is to have a true friend.

One day, having just left the room of Kōzuki Rōshi[5] (who also happened to be president of the university at the time) and walking along the corridor that leads back to the meditation hall, the sound of the bell of rejection still ringing in his hears, young Mumon noticed a ginkgo tree in the garden. When his eyes fell on its bright yellow leaves the young Mumon felt himself enter a state of "body and mind dropped off."[6] He felt himself one with the yellow ginkgo leaves. It was an impressive awakening to the realm where "things

---

[5] Kōzuki Tesshū 神月撤宗 (1879-1937) was superintendent of the Myōshin-ji branch of Rinzai Zen and President of Hanazono University.

[6] Dōgen is said to have had his experience of enlightenment after hearing his Chinese master, Ju-ching, use this phrase.

and I are one," a self-awareness of what Zen calls the "true person of no rank." This was the start of Mumon Rōshi's real entry into Zen.

He had been commuting faithfully back and forth between the master's bell and pondering his kōan,[7] but it was only when his eyes opened to the "formless self" where "self and other are not two" by becoming one with the yellow ginkgo tree in the garden that he realized Hakuin's Great Matter: that the transindividual and the individual are distinct but inseparable. He had walked through the Dharma gate of "non-duality." For the first time Mumon Rōshi became a Zen disciple awakened to the Original Self — to what I call "in a single breath, the transindividual individual."

TRUE PERSON AND TRUE SUCHNESS — TOUCHING THE GROUND OF RELIGION

As we noted in the previous chapter, during the first "Zen-Christian Dialogue," Yamada Mumon Rōshi compared his own experience to that of Yagi: "This is not something peculiar to me — Yagi said the same thing. It is an experience that touches the very foundations of religion, be it Buddhist or Christian." What can such an experience be? When Mumon Rōshi looked at the yellow leaves of the ginkgo tree and Yagi looked out the train window in Kassel at the woods, they both awakened to something. What was it they *saw*? Let us first recall the question Yagi put to himself:

> I have seen "true suchness." . . . Up until now, I had always thought a tree was a tree. Where did I go wrong?

In his own answer, Yagi explains that when we look at something concrete like a plum tree standing in front of us, its true suchness is hidden from us, dissipated into social conventions that take precedence over the actual tree itself. The concrete subject of the statement, "This plum tree is a plum tree" becomes swallowed up in the

[7] This is called "kōan *samādhi*."

abstract predicate. This was the way Yagi made rational sense of what he had experienced.

If I may be allowed to try to put this in my own words, it is because the ego is the seeing subject that true suchness gets eclipsed. "Social convention" is another name for the discriminating ego. In the experience of *dhyāna* — a meditative experience referred to variously as no-ego, no-mind, or *samādhi* — the ego is dropped off together with the world of discrimination it fashions. In its place, a world is opened up in which the "true person" *sees* "true suchness" (a completely new existence, the true face of the dharmas). This is the experience of transcendence or self-awareness called no-ego, no-mind, original self, in which what is seen by the new subject is the "such-as-it-is-ness" of reality. In this sense, religious experience may be understood as the appropriation of a dropped-off ego and the realization of an original, formless self. It is this true person who is then seeing and hearing true suchness. This is what Bashō celebrates in his image of the splash of water as the frog leaps into an old pond, or in the following verse:

> Look closely, you will see
> The flower on the hedge
> Of mother's-heart is blooming.

It is that of which the Christian scripture says:

> Behold, all things are become new! [2 Cor. 5:17]

All such statements point to an opening of the world of true suchness. This is what Mumon Rōshi means by "an experience that touches the very foundations of religion, Buddhist or Christian."

WHO GIVES THINGS NAMES?

Yagi, you will recall, also spoke of the problem of language. As social conventions, propositions like "This plum tree is a plum tree" also entail words. Human beings are born from the very beginning into a world of language. In the Old Testament story, everything the first man and woman encountered were completely new to them. The

Garden of Eden was already filled with things — in Buddhism we would call them dharmas — like mountains and rivers, trees and sky and clouds, when Adam came on to the scene. God then brought him his new creations one by one "to see what name he would give them." Adam looked at these *completely new things* — in Buddhist terms, we would say he looked at their true suchness — and gave them each a name.

With us it is different. As bearers of the original sin for which paradise was lost, we are born into a world of words. First we learn the words, then their conceptual meaning, and only *know* through the medium of those concepts what a "plum tree" is. Adam, as the first man, was able to contact things in their stark newness before he gave them names. This raw, original novelty is what Buddhism calls true suchness; it is also what Adam saw in the Garden of Eden. The "first man" of the Judeo-Christian tradition, or what Zen Buddhism calls the "true person," has no ego and therefore does not discriminate. For he had not yet eaten of the tree of "knowledge."

But the first man sinned. Following the woman who had been tempted by the serpent, a messenger of the devil, the man followed to eat of the "forbidden fruit." By eating of the tree of knowledge, human beings became an ego that discriminates — they became bearers of original sin.

"Which is more important for you, God or me?" Faced with this question from Eve, Adam must have thought to himself, "But of course, God is more important," but the answer he gave to her was, "You are." And so it was that the whole human race thereafter came to be burdened with the weight of original sin. Adam and Eve were given the ability to see things just as they are, but once they had tasted of the forbidden fruit of knowledge, the names they affixed to things were no longer attached to the true suchness of things.

This is what Buddhism refers to as *vijñāna* or discriminating knowledge, which is ultimately the work of the ego. We may think that such knowing brings us into contact with things in their newness or true suchness, but in fact we have not left the workings of the ego. As long as we remain there, surrounded by the discriminations learned at our mother's knee, at kindergarten, through primary school, high school, and university, the world of *satori* and the non-discriminating wisdom of *prajñā* remains closed to us.

Who then is the one to give the things that exist their proper names? Not the ego who is the subject of *vijñāna*, but only the original self who is the subject of *prajñā*. Only a new Adam and Eve, true persons who have regained the paradise lost, can do so. After his experience in the train at Kassel, Yagi came to appreciate these things, gained a good understanding of Buddhism, and brought the "eye of the heart" (the wisdom-eye of *prajñā*) to bear on his own study of Christian theology.

Over the past ten years, I have become close friends with Yagi and we have kept up our Christian-Buddhist dialogue. I recall once putting the question to him, "What is the most important thing that you, as a Christian, have learned from Buddhism?" Without a second thought, he replied at once, "Zen's *non-reliance on words*."

What can it mean for a Christian to accept Zen's claim of a direct transmission from mind to mind not relying on words? The meaning of Yagi's religious experience in the train at Kassel consists in an *awakening* to the grave error of trying to see and understand "things" by first having the "words" to give them a "conceptuality" apart from their concrete reality (social convention, discrimination). This sort of inversion of "existence" (the true face of dharmas, their true suchness) is also at work when a Christian gives the *words* of the Bible precedence over the *things* of existence, filtering the true suchness of things through "what the scriptures tell us." In vigorous protest against this sort of faith and theology, Yagi has continued to insist that the ineluctable existential *facts* of human existence take precedence over *words*. This in turn requires a second look at the meaning of theology in the intellectual history of the world.

Heretofore, ideas have been given precedence over reality, words have turned around to shape facts. Is this not precisely what the *Heart Sūtra* means by "mind-coverings"? In the words of Zen Master Mumon Ekai:

Words do not expand on things; language adds nothing to an event. Those who accept the words lose out; those who get arrested by the phrasing have gone astray.[8]

For Yagi as for me, Zen's "non-reliance on words" is its most important meaning for religion. What if one were to rethink Christianity in those terms? As the poet Okamoto Kanoko says:

> The plum flower blooms on the plum tree.
> It is no simple matter
> To see what this says to us.[9]

In chapter 3, I alluded to the problems posed by Toynbee and Jaspers regarding the dialogue between Christianity and Buddhism and the coming together of the knowledge of the West with the wisdom of the East. As to the former, I believe that we have gone a long ways towards making the dialogue a reality. We have come to a clear and mutual appreciation of the common foundations our two religious ways share.[10] The next step is to begin discussing what is fundamentally *different* about our two religions. Only then, bringing together the knowledge and wisdom of East and West, can we join in the common pledge to discipline and hard study that is needed to inaugurate a new future for humanity.

[8] Mumon Ekai 無門慧開 (1183-1260) was a leading Zen Master of Sung China and author of the *Mumonkan*.

[9] The poet Okamoto Kanoko 岡本かの子 (1889-1939) was noted for her passionate writing about the power of the feminine. Her collected works were published posthumously in 15 volumes.

[10] Among contributions to the dialogue Akizuki mentions explicitly (in addition to those already mentioned in earlier notes) are the following: Takizawa Katsumi 滝沢克己 , [*Where Art Thou?*] (Tokyo: San'ichi Shobō, 1983); Takizawa Katsumi and Yagi Seiichi, ed., 神はどこで見出されるか [*Where is God to be Found?*] (Tokyo: San'ichi Shobō, 1977); Yagi Seiichi and Abe Masao, ed., 仏教徒 キリスト教 [*Buddhism and Christianity*] (Tokyo: San'ichi Shobō, 1981); Yagi Seiichi and Akizuki Ryōmin, キリスト教の誕生 [*The Birth of Christianity*] (Tokyo: Seidosha, 1985), and 歴史のイエスを語る [*The Historical Jesus*] (Tokyo: Shunjūsha, 1984).

The Renewal of Practice

13 Towards a Fully
"Lay Buddhism"

THE DEPARTURE OF THE ELDEST SON

Recently I read through Miura Kiyohiro's novel, *The Departure of the Eldest Son*, winner of the 1988 Akutagawa Prize for literature. The story is narrated in the first person by a university professor of English who had worked his way through school in a United States university and returned to Japan in his thirties to marry and settle down. During his student years he had been asked by a young American, "What is Zen?" Unable to come up with an answer, he invented something on the spot. The memory of that event left a deep impression on him. One day, while walking in the neighborhood where he lived, he came upon a Zen temple and in no time found himself doing *zazen*. Early Sunday mornings, while the children were still asleep, he would go off to the temple to meditate. Not surprisingly, his wife did not take kindly to the idea. Nor did the children, who looked forward to playing with their father on Sunday. His son turned delinquent, pilfering food in the neighborhood and getting in trouble with a gang of his friends. Blamed by his wife for what was happening, the man turned to the nearby temple for advice.

As it turns out, the temple bonze in the story was a woman, a person of such experience and self-confidence that one cannot help feeling the character must be based on a real person. Anyway, she advises the protagonist of the story to bring his son along to the *zazen* sessions. At first, the boy simply played around and did not take things seriously. When some of the others began to complain that he was interfering with their efforts at *zazen*, the woman bonze cried out at them, "What good is a *zazen* so shallow that it gets distracted by a child at play?"

As time went on, the lad began to meditate with the others. In the beginning he tired quickly and would begin to fuss and fidget, but as time progressed, his sittings grew longer and longer until he was sitting as long as the adults. Unlike the other children, who looked forward to Sundays as a chance to play with their friends, the boy would wake his sleeping father and accompany him to the temple. Then one day, when he was in the third grade, he blurted out suddenly, "I want to become a bonze." As the story goes on, the boy, the "eldest son" of the title, actually does leave home in middle school to take up residence in a temple. The novel recounts how he breaks ties with his parents, leaves home, and—in a particularly impressive section—how he goes through the formalities of being ordained a monk. The image of the mother who has been left behind by her son is one of the more unforgettable sections of the book.

A review of the book by Gotō Akio in one of the evening papers had the following to say:

> It is not easy to see what the point of the novel is. After the ordination ceremony, the protagonist tells his son of his experience in the United States and reminds him that the Zen he has chosen is not the only Zen there is. Are we to take this to mean that the son's *departure into homelessness* means no more to his father than *leaving home?*[1]

I have to say, I was surprised to find someone like Gotō dismiss the work so curtly in this manner. From start to finish, it seems a rather ill-tempered review with an excess of animus against a work that

---

[1] *Asahi shinbun*, March 14, 1988. Gotō Akio 後藤明生 is a popular Japanese literary critic. In Japanese, the terms we have rendered as *leaving home* and *departure into homelessness* use the same characters in inverted order (家出, 出家). It should also be noted that the latter term is also a common term for a monk.

had, after all, been awarded the Akutagawa Prize. As a disciple of Zen, I would like to stand in for the novelist, Miura Kiyohiro — who graduated from the creative writing department of Iowa State University and is at present professor at the Meiji University of Industrial Arts — to attempt a more sympathetic and warmer review of the novel and its theme.

My wider motive for taking up the novel in the context of this book has to do with the general lack of understanding of matters religious among the intelligentsia of this country. The appearance of such a review makes us realize how much is wanting in proper awareness of what the monk's "departure into homelessness" means for Buddhism, both in its original sense and in the sense it has in contemporary Japan.

MAHĀYĀNA BUDDHISM IS NECESSARILY A "LAY BUDDHISM"

The New Mahāyāna I have been advocating in these pages has grown out of my own painful awareness of the demands facing Buddhism today, both from within and from without. Let us begin with the problems facing Buddhism from without.

The world has today entered into a new, post-modern age and this imposes strong demands on Buddhism if it intends to be part of this reality. In the preceding chapters, I addressed questions of the Christian-Buddhist dialogue and "New Age Science" from a Buddhist standpoint. My aim was to show that the idea of the ego taken over from modern Europe since the Meiji era has in fact become a "sickness unto death" for humanity at large, and that this makes it all the more critical that our Buddhist idea of the "ego of no-ego" be taught to the world.

Meantime, one of the problems facing Buddhism from within is to recognize that the need for something *new* in the Mahāyāna tradition is at the same time the need for a *true* Mahāyāna. In Buddhism, reformation is always restoration, and the New Mahāyāna's call for a "return to Śākyamuni" is no exception. When I speak of New Mahāyāna, therefore, my first idea is to "carry out the Mahāyāna spirit." I consider it vital for the thirty sects and fifty odd branches of Japanese Buddhism to return to Śākyamuni, to let go of traditions in their present state and reconsider the Buddhism of their own founders from the starting point of Buddhism.

But *which* Śākyamuni are we to return to? Surely *not* the Śākyamuni of the "scholars of primitive Buddhism" who tell us that "Mahāyāna Buddhism is an anti-Buddhist teaching." Such a view of Śākyamuni is a distortion, refracted through the glasses of the modern "ego". Mahāyāna is anything but an "anti-Buddhist theory." It is a teaching based immediately on the original words of the Buddha, a legitimate development of the "original form of Buddhism." This is the only standpoint from which, through dialogue among the various sects of Buddhism as well as through dialogue with Christianity, we can shed our skins for a new religious form. Our goal is to build a Buddha land on earth that is not only "intellectual" but also "historical." This is what makes the New Mahāyāna both *new* and *true* Mahāyāna.

Moreover, the Mahāyāna spirit must of necessity be a "lay Buddhism." In its origins, the Mahāyāna movement was a withdrawal from the élite Buddhism of the monastic minority and an attempt to bring "salvation to all sentient beings" by practicing the ideal of compassion that is the true spirit of Śākyamuni. The original Mahāyāna spirit was not restricted to a minority of homeless monks but took as its task the salvation of the lay masses. True to these origins, Mahāyāna Buddhism cannot *but* be a lay Buddhism.

In order to be fully lay, our New Mahāyāna must be "carried out" as a lay Buddhism. This means that the matter of practicing the Precepts is crucial. What is needed above all in this regard is a radical awareness of what it is that makes Mahāyāna the Great Vehicle, namely, the "sheer, unattached mind of Great Compassion." These two questions will occupy us in the chapters that follow.

Mahāyāna Buddhism refers to the *sangha* of Śākyamuni as "the harmonious union of four groups," by which it means the men and women who have gone into homelessness, *bhikku* and *bhikkuni*, and men and women lay believers, *upāsaka* and *upāsikā*. Clearly this is a very broad sense of the term *saṅgha*. In Buddhism's early period, even though the idea of the harmonious union of the four groups existed, the meaning of the *saṅgha* was restricted to the community of the *bhikku* and *bhikkuni*. This meant that there was a kind of division of labor in Śākyamuni's community between the monks and nuns who followed the example of Śākyamuni to leave home for homelessness, and ordinary lay men and women believers. The former left society and renounced a worldly trade in order to seek the Buddha Dharma through the strict preservation of the rules of the *vinaya*. Their renunciation of a place in the social system at large meant that they would not be able to secure food, and clothing, and housing for themselves and thus that they would have to rely entirely on donations from lay believers. At the same time, having no home to care for and no occupation to work at, the members of the *saṅgha* were able to keep both feet planted in the world of religious practice. In contrast, lay believers had to see to both home and occupation, and thus had to straddle the worlds of religious practice and worldly duties. In the long run, the practice of the monks would become more important, and it was their appropriation of the Dharma that would be passed on in turn to lay believers. This is what is known as the "donation of the Dharma." In exchange, the laity would share with the homeless the fruits of their labors in the world. This was called the "donation of goods." The harmony of the four groups thus took shape through the mutual sharing of the Dharma and goods.

In their practice of the Dharma of Śākyamuni, the homeless monks and nuns also strove to appropriate the Dharma intellectually. Their philosophical speculations about the teachings of the Buddha are known as *Abhidharma* (literally, "about the Dharma"). In this way, pure and clear teachings of Śākyamuni passed by way of deep contemplation into more and more systematic formulations, until at last they fell into the logical fineries of a highly analytical philosophy. Meantime, Śākyamuni's mind of Great Compassion that inclines to *prajñā* got derailed along the way. The Buddha Dharma turned into a topic of debate among a special élite all but cut off from the masses of ordinary people. From there it dispersed into a diversity of scholarly sects.

Against this backdrop, Mahāyāna Buddhism can be seen as a reform movement aimed at restoring the true significance of Śākyamuni that had been lost in the rise of sectarian Buddhism. The Mahāyāna movement did not arise from within the *saṅgha* in the narrow sense of the community of monks and nuns, but from among the community of lay believers known as the *gana*, a community of laity centered about the stūpa of Śākyamuni. A small group of progressive homeless leaders joined with the *gana* to form the Mahāyāna movement. From the very start, therefore, Mahāyāna was a lay Buddhist movement.

The Buddhist monks of the Southern Theravāda branch continue to this day to preserve the *vinaya* of the *bhikku saṅgha* from the time of early Buddhism. Theirs is essentially a "precept Buddhism," a "monk-and-temple" Buddhism. The homeless monks keep a different set of precepts than lay believers, which accounts for the strict distinction between lay and monastic. This does not mean that the *saṅgha* is cut off from society, withdrawn to some secluded forest or mountain. It is very much a part of society at large. Anyone can become a *bhikku* and enter the *saṅgha*, and even after becoming a *bhikku*, one is always free to return home. Returning to the lay state does not carry with it any stigma of religious backsliding. Far from being looked down upon, people who doff their saffron-colored robes after several decades to return to society are held in esteem by people in general for the years they spent in the monastic life. For better or for worse, Southern Theravāda Buddhism is a Buddhism of monks and temples. But if one therefore expects to find a higher level of morality among individual monks and a higher reverence for asceticism, one's expectations are bound to be frustrated.

Things are different with Buddhism here in Japan. We may speak of monks as "homeless ones," but in fact, as we explained in the opening chapter, they are really a kind of "laity-called-monks." Japanese Buddhism does not draw a sharp line of distinction between the homeless and the lay, although the mistaken expectation that there *should* be some such distinction continues to hang on. This helps explain the widespread confusion between "leaving home" and "departure into homelessness" which we saw in the book review cited earlier.

In any case, the reality of Buddhism as it is lived in Japan today leaves us with the question of whether or not we are in fact Buddhist if we do not have the kind of monk-and-temple precept Buddhism to be found in Southern Theravāda Buddhism. Is it not in fact impossible to practice the Buddhist path without at least keeping up the appearance of a homeless monk or nun? Is it realistic to talk about attaining *satori* without a departure into homelessness?

Absolutely not. Buddhist practice is no less possible for the laity than for the monk. *Satori* knows of no distinction between being at home and being homeless. This should be clear already from the fact that Mahāyāna Buddhism was originally a lay movement. Let there be no doubt: the teachings of Śākyamuni on *prajñā* and *karuṇā* belong not only to the *bhikku* who have left home but can also be appropriated in an outstanding way by the laity.

In considering what this New Mahāyāna of ours does, we must keep in mind that 99% of the monks in Japan today are actually "laity-called-monks." Only by first recognizing their *de facto* lay state can monks and laity work together for a Buddhism suited to the post-modern world. As I have said, this does not eliminate the need for specialists in some sense of the term, and indeed I would like to see more monks, fully aware of their lay state, standing in the vanguard of a New Mahāyāna where "monks and laity are one body."

THE PRAJÑĀ CHANT IN THE NEW MAHĀYĀNA

Enough about what has to be said. I would like to conclude with a word about what needs to be *done*. As I explained earlier, my own understanding of the main direction a New Mahāyāna has to take begins from the idea that "*prajñā* is *pāramitā*." Its "starting point" is a "return" to the *prajñā* Dharma of Prince Shōtoku; it follows Shinran in a profound descent into individuality; it takes from Nichiren the goal of constructing a Buddha land; and from Dōgen's theory of "true enlightenment, wondrous practice" it appropriates the idea of a Buddha Dharma that permeates all things.[2]

Since writing In Praise of Lay Zen, I have advocated the recitation of Mahāprajñāpāramitā while seated in the posture of Zen meditation. I see in this simple practice, which anyone can do, a crystallization of the whole of Mahāyāna Buddhism. Shaku Jōkō Rōshi replaced the chant of the patriarch Seizan Rōshi, "Namu shinjin prajñāpāramitā," with "Mahāprajñāpāramitā," claiming that he was trying to "draw a single target for the chanting of the prajñā Dharma." To this I merely added the qualification that it can be chanted "seated in the posture of Zen meditation." Hōnen and Shinran chanted the nenbutsu while Nichiren stressed "chanting the title (of the Lotus Sūtra)." As a practice for New Mahāyāna Buddhism, I am advocating the chanting of prajñāpāramitā. And that, it seems to me, is enough for Buddhism.

Why should I consider the chanting of the phrase prajñāpāramitā to be sufficient by itself? Simply because I find the "origins of Buddhism" in the self-awareness and living out of the original self.

Here I would like to repeat the teaching of Zen Master Bankei, the one monk I find most congenial to my own position, on the "Unborn Buddha mind." In his stress on the Unborn Buddha mind, Bankei preached "faith" in the fact that "sentient beings are originally Buddha." His was a straightforward and singleminded creed: the original self of human beings is "Buddha," or, put in traditional terms, "All sentient beings have the Buddha-nature." Let us cite Bankei's own words at length:

> Not a single one of you in attendance here today is an unenlightened person. You're a gathering of Unborn Buddha minds. If anyone thinks, "No, I'm not. I'm not enlightened," I want him to step forward. Tell me: What is it that makes a person unenlightened?

[2] See above, 32-34.

In fact, there are no unenlightened people here. Nonetheless, when you get up and begin to file out of the hall, you might bump into someone in front of you as you cross over the threshold. Or someone behind you might run into you and knock you down. When you go home, your husband, son, daughter-in-law, servant, or someone else may say or do something that displeases you. If something like that happens, and you grasp onto it and begin to fret over it, sending the blood to your head, raising up your horns, and falling into illusion because of your self-partiality, the Buddha-mind turns willy-nilly into a fighting spirit. Until you transform it, you live just as you are in the Unborn Buddha mind; you aren't deluded or unenlightened. The moment you do turn it into something else, you become an ignorant, deluded person. All illusions work the same way. By getting upset and favoring yourself you turn your Buddha-mind into a fighting spirit—and fall into a deluded existence of your own making.

So whatever anyone else may do or say, whatever happens, leave things as they are. Don't worry yourself over them and don't side with yourself. Just stay as you are, right in the Buddha-mind, and don't change it into anything else. If you do that, illusions don't occur and you live constantly in the Unborn mind. You're a living, breathing, firmly established Buddha. Don't you see? You have an incalculable treasure right at hand.[3]

My idea of practice for the New Mahāyāna in ordinary, everyday life consists simply in striving not to turn the "Unborn Buddha mind" into ordinary mind (the hellish mind, the mind of the hungry ghost, the beastly mind, the mind of the fighting spirit), but to spend the days of one's life in the "original purity" of the Unborn Buddha mind and devote one's every effort to living each day as a living Buddha. Shōju called this "determining the right mind" and "inheriting

---

[3] *The Unborn: The Life and Teaching of Zen Master Bankei, 1622-1693*, trans. by Norman Waddell (San Francisco: North Point Press, 1984), p. 39. The orthography has been adjusted to the conventions of the present text.

the right mind."[4] The same idea runs like a single thread throughout Hakuin's systematic practice of the kōan. Different religious leaders use different language, but all are getting at the same Great Matter.

If you have followed me this far, there should be no obstacle to "intoning *Mahāprajñāpāramitā* while seated in the posture of Zen meditation." One could just as well chant the name of the Buddha or of a sūtra. All who have found peace of mind in their own sect can direct that peaceful mind to a return to the direct teaching of Śākyamuni, the *prajñā* Buddha Dharma that is the "fountainhead of Buddhism," and participate in the New Mahāyāna movement after the manner of their own particular tradition.

THE NEW MAHĀYĀNA AT HOME AND AT WORK

In addition to the concrete practice of intoning *Mahāprajñāpāramitā*, I would like to advocate as part of the New Mahāyāna an imitation of Suzuki Shōsan's ideal of "making one's own work the activity of the Buddha." His ideas of "lay Zen" and a Buddhist "work ethic" are laid out in a work entitled *Meritorious Way of Life for All*.[5]

Shōsan was a follower of the Zen way who stressed that "More important than the Buddha one becomes after death is to live and work freely in the here and now." For him, "The true Buddha Dharma consists in being useful to society." Thus he stresses "becoming Buddha in the Dharma of the world" and insists that "if the Buddha Dharma does not make use of the society of people just as it is, it is not a true Buddha Dharma." In a word, Shōsan sees the Buddha Dharma as "a treasure to be spent in everyday life."

Because he taught that "the Buddha Dharma is the Dharma of society," Suzuki was also able to teach that peasants plowing their fields, artisans fashioning their wares, and merchants plying their

---

[4] Shōju Etan 正受慧端 , 1642-1721) was one of the masters of Hakuin. He is treated in chapter 14 below.

[5] This work is treated, with a generous selection of direct quotations, in chapter 9 of Winston King's *Death Was His Kōan: The Samurai Zen of Suzuki Shōsan* (Berkeley: Asian Humanities Press, 1986).

trade already in hand have their way to become a Buddha. Particularly significant for us in the present world is Shōsan's view of an "occupation." "The merchant," he says, is "an apostle of 'freedom'," since by taking things that are in one place and moving them to another, the merchant works to remove the unfreedom of people. Viewed from the standpoint of the *Lotus Sūtra*, that ". . . all are not distinct from true reality itself,"[6] the heart of Mahāyāna is more present in a Buddhism at home than a Buddhism that is homeless.

Shōsan writes:

> Dedicate your body to the world and with all your powers
> consider how to achieve the welfare of the country and all its
> people. Traveling about the country, conveying your goods
> from one province to another, from near and far, vowing that
> you will measure up to the expectations of everyone, you are
> practicing what is necessary to work off your karmic hin-
> drances. With this mind, cross mountains, apply yourself
> heart and soul, cleanse your mind as you cross rivers great
> and small. And when you set your craft afloat on the sea's
> wide expanse, cast off this body of yours and recite the
> *nembutsu*, remembering that a life is but a journey in this
> transitory world. If you abandon all attachments and put
> away greed, the heavens will protect you and the gods will
> favor you with a prosperous life; you will excel in making
> profits, and be so filled with prosperity that you will look
> down upon the chief men of great hereditary wealth. In your
> walking, standing, sitting, and lying down your mind will be
> at rest. Naturally and without effort the Buddha mind will be
> realized; becoming a person of unobstructed freedom, the
> freedom of *nirvāṇa*'s marvelous joy, you will walk along in the

[6] The phrase as quoted could not be located in the *Lotus Sūtra*. The context reads, in Hurvitz's translation, "The room of the Thus Come One is the thought of great compassion toward all living beings. The cloak of the Thus Come One is the thought of tender forbearance and the bearing of insult with equanimity." See *Scripture of the Lotus Blossom of the Fine Dharma* (New York: Columbia University Press, 1976), 180. See the tenth chapter of the *Lotus Sūtra*, T 9.31c25.

universe, joyous through endless future ages. What can
equal this! Work on, work on, with steadfastness![7]

I would note, parenthetically, that in an earlier book, I took issue
with the noted critic Yamamoto Shichihei, who wrote in his book
The Spirit of Japanese Capitalism that "Zen and the economic animal
stem from the same idea." My remarks were quickly taken up by
Yamaori Tetsuo, one of Japan's foremost religious critics.[8]

The practice of chanting *Mahāprajñāpāramitā* seated in the posture of Zen meditation, which I am advocating for the New
Mahāyāna, looks simple enough, but rests on an idea of the Buddha
Dharma whose origins are old and deep. But if the "wellsprings of a
new Buddhism" as I understand it indeed reach back to the *satori* of
Śākyamuni himself, then we need also to look for a "new dogmatics"
to accompany the practice of the New Mahāyāna, a truly "post-
modern, all-in-one Buddha Dharma."

---

[7] See King, *Death Was His Kōan*, 246-51.

[8] Akizuki is referring here to his book *In Praise of Lay Zen* (see above, 33, n.12).
Yamamoto Shichihei 山本七平 is perhaps best known outside of Japan as the
anonymous author of *The Japanese and the Jews* (Tokyo: Weatherhill, 1973). The
work referred to here is 日本資本主義の精神 (Tokyo: Kōbunsha, 1984).
Yamaori Tetsuo 山折哲雄 , currently engaged at the International Research
Center for Japan Studies in Kyoto, is a well-known authority on Japanese religious
ethnology.

14 The Precepts in the New Mahāyāna

SHOULD MONKS BE ALLOWED TO MARRY AND EAT MEAT?

The final article in the fivefold prayer I introduced back in chapter 3 read: "To revere the true way of homelessness and bring about a new lay Buddhist way." The establishment of a new lay Buddhism cannot avoid the challenge of keeping the precepts, and it is to this question that I would turn my attention next.

Among my many Buddhist-priest friends is a first-rate Buddhist scholar who suffers acutely from the tension of having been ordained a priest and yet being married and eating meat. Because of the tension, he finds himself inhibited from committing himself fully to his work as a priest. For those in the tradition of Shinran, the problem has already been taken care of, since Shinran taught a radical stance of "neither priest nor lay." Priests in this line are free to go about their priestly duties with nothing to worry about. But matters are not so easy for those in other Buddhist schools. In many cases, the more dedicated and serious the priest, the more he is sure to feel the pain of the contradiction.

When Yōsai[1] transmitted the Ch'an tradition from China, he brought with it the Sung period Chinese attitude toward the pre-

---

[1] Also known as Eisai 栄西 (1141-1215), the transmitter of the Rinzai Zen tradition to Japan.

cepts, which remains in effect, at least formally, in Japan today. This ideal, "the practice of both Mahāyāna and Hīnayāna precepts," means that all Zen priests in Japan are ordained under the Hīnayāna *bhikku* precepts. Little wonder that my scholar-priest friend should suffer the shame and tension he does.

Speaking as one within the Zen tradition, I believe that the only necessary precepts are the "precepts of the formless mind."[2] Here I follow the lead of Saichō, the founder of Japanese Tendai Buddhism, who favored the "Mahāyāna rule alone." For him, the Mahāyāna bodhisattva precepts were enough for ordination to the priesthood. There was no need to follow the Hīnayāna *bhikku* precepts also. I should add that my teacher, Yamada Mumon Rōshi, as well as my revered mentor, Morimoto Shōnen Rōshi, both opposed me on this point. For both of them, the Hīnayāna precepts were included within the Mahāyāna precepts. Still, I remain firm in my resolve to find a place for the Japanese Tendai practice of "Mahāyāna rule alone" within Japanese Zen also.

Dōgen also sided with Saichō in considering the Mahāyāna rule sufficient. His master, Myōzen, had been ordained in Nara before going to Sung China, and was accepted as a monk in the Zen monasteries of China. In contrast, Dōgen, who rejected the Hīnayāna precepts of the Nan-shan tradition and accepted only the "Mahāyāna rule alone" of Japanese Tendai, was not recognized as a monk in Sung China. In spite of this, Dōgen never compromised his convictions. The difference between Dōgen and me is that, in actual practice, Dōgen kept the Hīnayāna precepts in daily life, while I accept only the Mahāyāna bodhisattva precepts in both theory and in the practice of daily life.

Strictly speaking, the only indispensable precepts for the follower of the Zen are "the precepts of the formless mind." Everything else is

---

[2] This phrase is an abbreviation of the term 無相金剛心地戒 , "the precepts of a mind which is hard as diamond and without form," which is often used in the Zen tradition to describe their attitude toward the precepts.

secondary. If I may cite a verse of Takamura Kōtarō, a disciple of Nishiyama Kasan Rōshi:[3]

> There is no path before me,
> Only the path I leave behind me as I go.

I see no need for the complicated and troublesome Hīnayāna rule. As Bankei said, "one who lives in the Unborn Buddha mind has no precepts." Keeping the precepts is a *spontaneous self-unfolding* of *prajñā*-wisdom. This, as I have remarked often in these pages, is what is meant by the "*pāramitā* of keeping the precepts," or what Dōgen called the "wondrous practice of original enlightenment."

Shōju taught that "there is no use bestowing the practice of the precepts on one who has not been enlightened." From this point of view, the current practice in the Hakuin tradition of having masters ordain their disciples runs counter to the spirit of Shōju and Hakuin. Even though they know full well that this is a deliberate infraction of their own tradition, they follow the Kogetsu tradition of seeing ordination as a "bond of affinity" between master and disciple.[4] As long as they are *aware of what they are doing*, I have no doubt that Hakuin and Shōju would nod approval from their state of nirvanic bliss.

IN PRAISE OF THE MAHĀYĀNA BODHISATTVA PRECEPTS

In my recent book, *In Praise of Lay Zen*, I endorsed the importance of accepting the precepts within daily life — a kind of ordination for everyday life — as these are understood in the Kogetsu tradition. My own view in this matter is that the understanding of precepts in the Shōju-Hakuin tradition is correct, but that the spirit of a Mahāyāna bodhisattva cannot always insist on such a strict attitude in the face of life as it is lived. Shōju might not agree with me on this point, but I am sure Hakuin would. Otherwise there would be no way for him

---

[3] Nishiyama Kasan 西山禾山 was a leading Zen master and a priest of Daihō-ji. Takamura Kōtarō 高村光太郎 was a distinguished modern poet.

[4] Kogetsu Zenzai (1677-1751) was the head of a now extinct Rinzai line opposing that of Hakuin.

to realize his commitment to the idea that "the noble deeds of the bodhisattva are the source of the Buddha land."

Dōgen's understanding of the precepts is best suited to passing on a "lived" acceptance of the precepts, and the easiest for contemporary people to accept. This was what I had in mind in publishing my lectures on the *Principles of Practice and Enlightenment in the Sōtō Order*.[5] In a word, this approach teaches that as soon as one is "ordained" to the precepts, one's originally pure self or Buddha-nature begins to work and one becomes at once "a child of all Buddhas," "on a par with the Great Awakening of the Buddha." When one accepts the precepts and vows to live as a Buddhist, come what may, one is given a Buddhist name (*kaimyō*),[6] and from that moment on seeks to live by the "Unborn Buddha mind."

Contrary to what is commonly believed in Japan, the *kaimyō* is not a name assigned at one's funeral after one has died, as a kind of passport to get you safely through the next world and into the paradisal land of ultimate bliss. When I proposed in *In Praise of Lay Zen* that one should be given the *kaimyō* while one is still alive, the idea was criticized by monks on the grounds that if such a practice were to become widespread, temple revenues from funeral expenses would suffer. But surely we must not allow ourselves to be dictated to by such base concerns and risk losing sight of the Great Matter of the Buddha Dharma.

The term *precepts* suggests to good men and women of the world a fastidious and vigilant morality that demands strict adherence to rules such as not eating meat or drinking alcoholic beverages, austere self-control, avoiding contact with the opposite sex, and so on.

One thinks here of the famous poem of Yosano Akiko:[7]

> You never feel loneliness teaching the Way,

---

[5] The work referred to (修証義) is a late nineteenth-century compilation of selections from Dōgen's *Shōbōgenzō*. See Akizuki's 正法眼蔵の奥義 [*The Inner Meaning of the Shōbōgenzō*] (Kyoto: PHP Kenkyūjo, 1985).

[6] 戒名 , literally a "precepts name."

[7] Yosano Akiko 与謝野晶子 was a famous poet of Meiji Japan.

nor the pulse of hot blood under soft skin!

(I am not sure if these lines were composed in praise of a Zen master or Catholic priest who remains pure in his task of teaching the truth, or if it is meant to express pity for those who have never tasted the joys of life.)

The laity are a fickle lot. On the one hand, they do as they please, and then on the other, they turn around and say, "Japanese priests all break the precepts, but the Buddhist priests of other countries are pure because they follow the Hīnayāna precepts." I urge such persons to take pride in their Mahāyāna heritage and confidently seek to live as bodhisattva "priests" themselves. The Mahāyāna rule is not concerned with things like eating meat or sleeping together. Its concern is with action that flows directly and naturally from a realization of *prajñā*-wisdom. Its aim is to promote commitment to the Mahāyāna bodhisattva vow to save all sentient beings. This is what Suzuki Daisetz Sensei meant when he wrote: "The *Lotus Sūtra* also speaks of the steadfast, unwavering diligence of the mind that acts with Great Compassion for the sake of all sentient beings."[8]

NON-IDENTIFIABLE, INSEPARABLE, IRREVERSIBLE

The supreme teaching of Buddhism is *Mahāprajñāpāramitā*. It is the doctrine *taught by* the Buddha as well as the doctrine about *becoming oneself* a Buddha. To become a Buddha means not only to awaken to *prajñā* and see into one's "original self," but also to make that insight actual (*pāramitā*) in daily life.

This is what we spoke of earlier as the twofold dynamic involved in the perfection of wisdom: the "uphill path" of ascent *to enlightenment* that moves from Precepts to Meditation to Wisdom, and the "downhill path" of descent *from enlightenment* that proceeds from Wisdom to Meditation to the Precepts. The former is known in Buddhism as the "first awakening" and the latter as the "original awak-

---

[8] The phrase that Akizuki cites here 不息不断 is a paraphrase of a passage in the *Lotus Sūtra*. For the reference to Suzuki's statement, see below, 185, n. 8.

ening."[9] The two forms of awakening are distinct from each other (*non-identifiable*), intimately bound to each other (*inseparable*), and sequentially determined (*irreversible*), in the sense that original enlightenment is prior to first enlightenment.

This latter point is critical. One's own awakening is always the self-authentication of a *basic fact* that seems to lie at the ground of the self of all people everywhere. This is why Dōgen can speak of the "marvelous cultivation of original enlightenment." Here is the source of the spontaneous, self-unfolding of *prajña*.

RELIGIOUS FORM AND ZEN FORMLESSNESS

The meaning of Dōgen's "just sitting" is that *zazen* is to be practiced not in order to become a Buddha, but in order that the Buddha within sentient beings might come to enlightenment in a spontaneous and self-unfolding manner, as the perfection of wisdom. In this sense seated meditation is not limited to sitting but includes the actualization of *prajña*-wisdom through the four basic functions of "going, staying, sitting, and lying down." This is the sense of the phrase cited earlier, "Noble deeds are the Buddha Dharma, doing the Dharma is the heart of the teaching." Everything we do becomes "just" doing ("the perfection of wisdom"-in-"the marvelous cultivation of original enlightenment"). As we have said, Zen is not just *samādhi*, one of the three elements of Buddhist doctrine. It is rather what Hui-neng called "the equality of *samādhi* and wisdom, the oneness of Zen and precepts." Here we have the real beginnings of Chinese Zen, or what I like to call the "Master's Zen" of China in contrast to the "Tathāgata's Zen" of India. The two are at once completely the same and completely distinct.

The *zazen* in which *sentient beings* seek to realize awakening is a "pre-*prajña*" *zazen*. In contrast, the *zazen* practiced by a *Buddha* is a *zazen* based on the perfection of *prajña*-wisdom; it is a "post-*prajña*"

[9] The corresponding Sino-Japanese terms are 始覚 and 本覚 . See also above, 91-94.

zazen. The same thing can be said of keeping the precepts. Precepts that are kept because one is obliged to keep them are what Hui-neng called "precepts of form." In contrast, precepts that are carried out as the working of the Buddha (one's original self or Buddha-nature) are "formless precepts." It is in following such formless precepts that one can say "There is no path before me, only the path I leave behind me as I go"; or in the words of Confucius: ". . . I could follow the dictates of my own heart; for what I desired no longer overstepped the boundaries of right."[10]

These formless principles, as Shōju never tired of saying, are the true precepts of the Zen way. They are Hakuin's *vinaya*. When Hakuin was twenty-four years old, in the second month of spring at Eigan-ji in Echizen, he had an experience of *satori* which he arrogantly described by saying, "In the past three hundred years, no one has had so marvelous an insight as I." In the fourth month of the same year he visited Shōju at Iiyama in the Shinshū area. Shōju disparaged his *satori* experience and put him through the rigors of practice all over again so that he might reach the true awakening of a Buddha.

In the fifth month of that year, while residing at Ekō-in in Matsumoto, Hakuin considered receiving the Hīnayāna precepts. Upon hearing of Hakuin's intent, Shōju immediately explained the "formless precepts" to the disciple and conferred these on him instead. Hakuin's biographer writes that Hakuin welcomed these precepts tearfully, at which Shōju remarked, "Our Zen way has the 'precepts of the formless mind' [the Mahāyāna bodhisattva Zen precepts] which have been passed down through the years from one patriarch to the next, all the way to me."[11] And with that, he expounded the "one-mind precepts" (or "self-nature precepts") of Bodhidharma and conferred them on his disciple.

This is of course the same Shōju whom we cited earlier as saying

---

[10] *The Analects of Confucius*, trans. by Arthur Waley (New York: Vintage, 1938), 88 (2.4).

[11] Hakuin's biography 白隠年譜 is attributed to Tōrei Enji 東嶺圓慈 .

that "There is no use bestowing the practice of the precepts on one who has not been enlightened." Elsewhere, we hear him remarking:

> This is the sage insight [*prajñā*-wisdom] of the Tathāgata; the Great Masters [buddhas] of the past, present, and future and in all directions have transmitted this body of precepts, and appeared in this world "riding on the wheel of their vows." If people wish to receive the precepts, they should seek insight. People without insight, even should they have the body of precepts, speak the language of delusion.

ZEN'S "PRECEPTS OF THE FORMLESS MIND"

The key to terms like "formless precepts," "precepts of the formless mind," "one-mind precepts," and "self-nature precepts" lies in the word *formless*. In the Shōju-Hakuin tradition, the meaning of this term is approached first by way of kōan. The "setting" is all important here. One must first have a direct experience of *becoming* formless oneself before one can utter so much as a single syllable about it. Thus one begins by accepting the precepts and living a life of self-control. With mind and body regulated, one learns to be calm and concentrated through the practice of *zazen*. One seeks to cultivate *samādhi* night and day, to enter a state of no-self in which mind and body are as one. This is the setting for "formlessness," the marvelous state in which for the first time one can experience the condition of no-self and no-mind in which the ego is truly emptied. The follower of the Zen way, if pressed to describe the experience of being in a state of "truly empty formlessness" can only say:

> There is no heaven and no earth, no self or others, no past and no present, no Buddha and no sentient beings, no passionate attachments and no liberating wisdom, no *saṃsāra* and no *nirvāṇa* — and yet neither is it that these things do *not* exist.

In the *Heart Sūtra*, the *negation*, "form (self) is emptiness," is immediately inverted to the *affirmation*, "emptiness is form (self)." This is what is meant by the saying, "To die and live — this is the way of Zen." It is a state of mind (Skt., *citta*) that reaches for *bodhi*-wisdom above and for the salvation of all sentient beings below. Formless mind is not a static state of *nirvāṇa* in which to enjoy the fruits of enlightenment. It is a dynamic state that impels a Buddha to become a bodhisattva and act on behalf of all sentient beings. Just as the earth gives rise to all things, so the formless mind is the "mind-ground" out of which all the wondrous deeds of the "one mind" arise to dispel the thoughts that fill the ordinary minds of ignorant fools. In the Shōju-Hakuin tradition, the inquiry into "formlessness–mind-ground–body of precepts" takes place in the "Dharma dialogue" between master and disciple facing each other, one on one, in a closed room.

As for the term *body of precepts*, there are those who have taken the word *body* to mean the physical body — "this bag of shit," as Lin-chi calls it — but that is to miss the point. If that were all it meant, then ideas like "mind-ground," "true emptiness — wondrous being," "death-and-resurrection," and so forth would be enough on their own. No, the "body of precepts" has to do with what Suzuki Daisetz Sensei called the "true emptiness — wondrous doing," of the "subject of absolute nothingness" (the activity of saving other sentient beings that arises from the unattached mind of Great Compassion).

In a word, the "precepts of the formless mind" refer to a person of deep insight, that is, to a Buddha, in whom the Great Wisdom of *prajñā* has become the bodhisattva's vow to Great Compassion and for whom practice has become diligent *prajñāpāramitā*. That is why Daisetz Sensei could speak of it as acting with unbroken and ceaseless diligence for the sake of all sentient beings. This is also where I locate the meaning of Dōgen's mysterious phrase, "the marvelous cultivation of original enlightenment." To empty the self and become completely empty is to step beyond duality. The wisdom of emptiness (selflessness) is a *realization of the original self that lies beyond the duality of self and others*. For here the pains and sufferings of all sentient beings become the self's own suffering and the self's own pain, and one cannot but exert oneself diligently for the benefit of others. This is the main thing I learned from Suzuki's Zen, and I shall return to it in the final chapter.

SERENITY IN ENLIGHTENMENT, SERENITY IN FAITH

In modern times, two conflicting views regarding the precepts have prevailed in Japanese Rinzai Zen. The first is that just discussed — the emphasis on "formless precepts" in the Shōju-Hakuin tradition. The other is the idea of "precepts as a bond of affinity" endorsed by Kogetsu Zenzai.

Hakuin, as we have seen, followed his master Shōju's teaching that persons lacking insight into the Buddha nature or realization of the unattached self were not to receive the precepts. For without the experience of the "one mind," how could one put into practice the keeping of precepts that are supposed to flow naturally from the formless mind? This assertion comes naturally for Zen, and I myself find nothing objectionable in it. But if the true "mind-ground precepts" do not function except for persons of such enlightened insight, what about all the people who have not yet attained insight? What are they to do to be saved? Unless we can answer *that* question, the Mahāyāna bodhisattva path is meaningless.

This is where Dōgen's idea of the precepts comes in. In Dōgen's own words:

> The World-Honored One [the Buddha] clearly pointed out to all sentient beings, "When sentient beings accept the Buddhist precepts, they enter into the realm of the Buddha — truly attaining the same awakening and becoming the children of the Buddha."[12]

The words Dōgen cites come from the *Mahāyāna Brahmajāla Sūtra*.[13] Although this is a Mahāyāna sūtra, Dōgen had no doubt that they were the words of Śākyamuni. In fact, for him, "*anyone* who attains

---

[12] The passage appears in the 伝衣 "Transmission of the Robe" chapter of Dōgen's *Shōbōgenzō*.

[13] See T 24.1484.

satori is Śākyamuni." In other words, "Buddha" refers to one who has perfected the "originally pure mind," who has realized the "original self." *Faith* in this religious fact, as the Buddha's words reveal, is the one Great Matter beyond all others. Hence the *Principles of Practice and Enlightenment in the Sōtō Order*, the text used by the Sōto Zen school for the past hundred years to spread their doctrine, encourages people to confirm themselves in their "faith" and to accept the "precepts" in order to "enter the realm of the Buddhas."

Seen strictly in terms of Hakuin's idea of "serenity in enlightenment" (the peace of mind that comes from authenticating one's Buddha-nature through a "first-enlightenment" experience), one cannot confer the formless precepts (the Mahāyāna precepts based on insight into *prajñā*-wisdom and emptiness) on a blind person (one whose mind's eye has not opened to enlightened insight). At the same time, we have Dōgen's idea of "serenity in faith" (the peace of mind that comes from believing in the words of the Buddha and in the religious reality to which his teachings point, and basing one's life on that belief). If the "wisdom" and "understanding" of *zazen* and enlightened insight are made the focal point of practice, the general populace cannot but feel distant from Zen. This is why I prefer to shift the focus to the "faith" and "sentiment" of accepting the precepts and entering the order. As practices, these seem to fulfill the Mahāyāna bodhisattva commitment to show all sentient beings the way to the Buddhist path.

This approach is also present in the modern-day Rinzai school, in particular, as the Kogetsu tradition's understanding of conferring the precepts. Priests in the Shōju-Hakuin tradition to this day participate in ceremonies for conferring the precepts in a spirit of Great Compassion, so that as many sentient beings as possible can feel ties to the Buddha Dharma. The practice is based on the belief, as just noted, that if sentient beings accept the precepts, they become "children of the Buddha" whose enlightenment is one with that of the Buddha. This is why Zen masters of the Shōju-Hakuin tradition deliberately break the practices of their own tradition.

The New Mahāyāna movement I am advocating endorses the idea

that anyone who comes to a sense of "faith" should go to a master without delay to receive the Mahāyāna precepts, to have a Buddhist name conferred on them, and from that day forward to live body and soul as a follower of the Buddha. The moment one accepts the precepts, one's inherent Buddha-nature (one's original self as a Buddha) is set in motion and a new "child of the Buddha" begins a life of the "wondrous cultivation of original enlightenment."

15 The Buddha's Teaching on Relentless Striving

THE FOOTPRINTS OF AN ELEPHANT

I have always considered Masutani Fumio's *One Hundred Buddhist Stories*[1] a classic work on early Buddhism and recommend it highly to everyone. I would like to open my final chapter with a story Masutani has extrapolated from three short Pāli *Āgama* texts, a story he calls "Like the Morning Sun in the Blue Sky — Relentless Striving."

The story opens with Śākyamuni standing in the Jeta Grove outside Sāvasti. He turns to his disciples and says:

> Monks, all the beings that walk the earth make their own footprints, but there is not a one of them that would not fit within the footprint of the elephant. The footprint of the elephant is the largest of all.

The image of animal tracks inside the footprints of an elephant is clearly Indian in origin. For people who live in a country where elephants roam about, there could hardly be a better metaphor for something that includes or contains everything else. But what is the Buddha trying to say? His next remarks make it clear that his aim is

[1] See above 77, n. 1.

to identify the greatest, most comprehensive form of religious practice.

> Monks, in the same way, there are many paths [of religious practice] in this world, but all are based on relentless striving. Therefore of all good things, relentless striving is the greatest and noblest.

As the compiler notes, the term *relentless striving* is not a common one in the annals of Japanese Buddhism. For some reason it never took root in Japanese society but languished as something of a dead letter in the Buddhist scriptures. At the risk of exaggeration, I would say that the recovery of this term as a central part of the Buddhist tradition in itself makes Masutani Sensei's book valuable.

CONCENTRATION AND CONTINUITY

The Japanese word for "relentless striving" is a compound of three Chinese characters.[2] The first character, *fu*, is a privative. The second element, *hō*, means to let go or neglect. It appears in the phrase we find in the Chinese *Book of Mencius,* "seeking the *released* mind," meaning regain a lost conscience. The final character, *itsu*, connotes divergence or deviation from a goal. Thus *hōitsu* means selfish or self-centered, and with the privative prefix added, "unselfish" or "not stubborn and intractable."

Masutani Sensei explains that the compound did not originally exist in Chinese but was invented to translate the Sanskrit Buddhist term *apramāda,* which means *vigilance* or *diligence.* In the Noble Eightfold Path, it takes the form of "correct effort."[3] Diligence is also one of the six *pāramitā* of Mahāyāna: charity, keeping the precepts,

---

[2] 不放逸 . Akizuki prefaces his analysis of the term with a brief comment on the role of Indian languages, classical Chinese, and Japanese in shaping modern Buddhist thought and practice. These remarks have been omitted from the English edition.

[3] Nakamura Hajime 中村 元 , 仏教語大辞典 [*Cyclopedia of Buddhist Terms*] (Tokyo: Tokyo Shoseki, 1981), 1172.

patience, diligence, meditation, and wisdom. Nakamura Hajime's standard reference work on Buddhist terms lists *fuhōitsu* as the Chinese translation of the Pāli term *appamāda* (Skt. *apramāda*), and defines it as "discipline without indolence," "a mind set on good and not easily swayed," and "concerted practice of the good." From its first beginnings and down through the Mahāyāna tradition, then, Buddhism has held the virtue of diligence in high esteem.[4]

Even with all this etymological help, we still need to clarify just *what* kind of diligence it is we are talking about. For Masutani Sensei, *fuhōitsu* is a diligence of *concentration and continuity*. It is a "vigilant" diligence, on guard against being distracted by things or becoming attached to them. Such "concentration" is of the utmost importance, since our best and most productive work is done when mind and body are concentrated in diligence.

In Buddhism the term "samādhi" is also used to mean "concentration." The Chinese translation used the character for "settled" or "established," thus giving the connotation of "establishing the mind, immobile, in one spot."[5] Another Chinese compound used to render the word carried the sense of ridding oneself of all discrimination and maintaining tranquility of mind. Thus *samādhi* has to do with a peaceful state of mind and body resulting from concentrating the mind.[6]

For Masutani Sensei, then, "relentless striving" refers to a form of diligence that values concentration and continuity, and seeks to avoid distractions and attachments. This is what the Buddha taught to be the greatest of all ways of practice:

> Any monk who strives relentlessly will cultivate the

---

[4] 禅 . The term 禅定 has much the same meaning, the only difference being the prefix of a character that translated the Sanskrit term *dhyāna.*

[5] 等持 . Incidentally, there is a Zen temple in Kyoto named after this term, Tōji-in.

[6] Akizuki notes that the sense of this term is more or less equivalent to two ordinary Japanese terms: "doing one's best" (一生懸命) and "single-minded" (一心不乱).

Noble Eightfold Path, and can look forward to its realization.

. . . .

Monks, innumerable countless stars shimmer in the night sky, but all of them put together do not amount to even a tenth of the moon's light. Thus moon is the greatest light in the night sky. In the same way, there are many paths in this world, but they are all based on relentless striving. Thus of all good deeds, relentless striving is the greatest and noblest.

Again, monks, when the sun rises in a cloudless autumn sky, all darkness is dispelled and light immediately shines in all directions. Of all the seasons of the year, the sun is said to shine most brightly against the autumn sky. In the same way, there are many paths in this world, but of them all, relentless striving is the most basic. Thus of all good deeds, relentless striving is the greatest and noblest.

There are as many religious paths as there are stars in the sky at night. But just as the moon outshines all the stars, so is the path of relentless striving the noblest of all paths. Similarly, we are made to imagine a cloudless autumn morning and to think of the sun rising against the deep blue of the sky as a metaphor for the highest of all paths. Indian scriptures often strike us Japanese as dry and wordy, and tend to make us feel out of place. But these metaphors are easy to understand. Surely the sermons of Śākyamuni were simple and beautiful like this! As we read such passages from early Buddhist texts, we get some sense of what it must have been like to sit and listen to the sermons of the Buddha 2,500 years ago in the Jeta Grove. This is the appeal of the early Buddhist texts that Masutani's superb translation has caught so well.

SAMĀDHI, DHYĀNA, AND HITSU-ZENDŌ

The combination of concentration and continuity brings to mind the Japanese discipline of *hitsu-zendō* — literally, the Zen way of the brush. Rather than an art form, *hitsu-zendō* is actually a form of meditation practiced by dipping a brush in black ink and drawing lines on a white sheet of paper to produce characters and words. The discipline began with Yokoyama Tenkei, who studied calligraphy in the Daishi branch of Juboku-dō, and Yamada Kensai, a disciple of Ōmori Sōgen. It was then picked up by Terayama Tanchū, and is to this day popular both in Japan and in Europe.[7] I myself studied very briefly at an early stage with Yamada Kenzai and can still recall what it felt like to dip the brush deeply into the ink and hold it still, poised over the pure white paper. Before making a mark one becomes "centered," mind and body as one, suspended in a state of mindfulness. But no sooner does a line of ink touch the paper to make a point than concentration fails. As one draws that single point out into a horizontal line, and then lifts the brush to add a vertical line, it becomes clearer and clearer that the sense of mindfulness is fading. The black lines on the paper are a portrait of that breakdown, there for all to see.

The experience is disconcerting to say the least. The concentration that one achieved prior to the contact of brush with paper is broken as soon as the dot breaks away to become a line. One is only too well aware of the inadequacy of the brush strokes, and one is able to tell with one's own eyes whether one's practice is doing any good or not. This is what makes *hitsu-zendō* so attractive as a discipline. In practicing *zazen* it is difficult to measure one's own progress, but with brush in hand one can *see* immediately how clear one's mind has become, how firm one's concentration has been.

The importance of achieving concentration and maintaining its continuity are of course important for *zazen* as well. Osaka Kōryū Rōkan always emphasized the practice of "*samādhi* power." He also talked of how truly enjoyable it is to breathe during *zazen*. Since *zazen* is an experience of "the concentration and serenity of body and mind," breathing exercises are practiced to concentrate and still body and mind. In other words, by regulating one's breathing one is able to control the concentration and tranquility of body and mind.

---

[7] These three figures, Yokoyama Tenkei 横山天啓 , his leading disciple Yamada Kensai 山田研斎 , and Terayama Tanchū 寺山旦中 are the most important figures in Japanese *hitsu-zendō* 筆禅道 .

This, too, is *samādhi*, the cultivation of motionless, undistracted mental concentration on one's breathing. Through it one is brought to a state in which one is concentrated on "breathing the mind," in which body and mind are centered and still. The power that accompanies this state is called "*samādhi* power," which one cultivates in order to achieve the goal of *bodhi*-wisdom or *satori*. This is why one begins with the practice of *zazen*. There is more involved here than merely setting aside specific times to sit in the proper cross-legged position. One must also be cultivating *samādhi* whenever one is "doing" *zazen* — that is, in all forms of daily life. This is what Śākyamuni meant by relentless striving, a diligent effort that serves not only as a prelude to the attainment of *prajñā*-wisdom but must also spill over into the most important practice of all, the practice *after* attaining *prājña*-wisdom.

SUZUKI DAISETZ SENSEI'S GREAT LESSON

When I read the term *relentlessly striving* in Masutani Sensei's book, my thoughts turned at once to my departed teacher, Suzuki Daisetz. From the time I first met him in the years immediately following the war until he passed away at the advanced age of ninety-six, I was in close contact with Suzuki Sensei for some twenty years. Unfortunately for me, he was abroad for about half of that time, but I was particularly fortunate to be at his side for his last seven and a half years, the mellowest of his life. The greatest lesson I ever learned from Suzuki Daisetz was "the *pāramitā* of diligence," which is precisely what Masutani Sensei meant by "relentless striving." It was Suzuki Daisetz Sensei who showed me the true meaning of "diligence that values concentration and continuity." Indeed, his whole life was a shining example of this teaching of the Buddha.

In a foreword to the second edition of my modern rendition of the record of Zen Master Jōshū, a work that was completed while I was studying under him, Suzuki Sensei wrote:

> One hardly need mention how crucial a study of the *Record of Jōshū* is. He is a figure no less important than Lin-chi,

Ummon, and Dōsan. There are those that find him insuffer-
able. As for me, I find deep sympathy with the spirit of a man
who can write, "May all people be reborn in heaven; may
none sink into the interminable sea of suffering of this
world." The *Lotus Sūtra* also speaks of the steadfast, unwavering diligence of the mind that acts with Great Compassion for the sake of all sentient beings. Jōshū may not have
the sting of the Zen stick or shout, but in this modern age of
science, mechanization, and organization we can ill afford to
forget his words: "I dumped thirty-five gallons of fresh ashes
on my head and aimed my practice first at saving others, but
now I have grown dull and forgotten what I had in mind."[8]

This is none other than the Buddha's teaching of relentless striving. It is the *pāramitā* of diligence. But there is another matter of
great moment here, namely, the *source* of the virtue of diligence and
relentless striving. How could the Mahāyāna bodhisattva Daisetz
Sensei live life to the fullest, in a spirit of steadfast, unwavering diligence, up until the final day of his ninety-six years? Only by virtue
of his bodhisattva "vow" to attain a "singleminded, unattached mind
of Great Compassion." That is the alpha and omega of everything
for him.

According to Matsubara Taidō Sensei,[9] Daisetz Sensei "worked in
a race against death." He knew he had a mission to accomplish, and
that mission was to communicate "the Mahāyāna Buddhist mind of
prajñā-wisdom" to the people of the world. Even when he was phys-
ically exhausted, he would go out of his way to greet visitors from
abroad. This was also his purpose behind his English commentary on
the Kegon Buddhist teachings and his final work, also in English, on
the original teachings of Buddhism.[10] All these labors were under-
taken in that same spirit of steadfast, unwavering diligence for the

---

[8] See Akizuki Ryōmin, 校訂国訳趙州禅師語録 *[Revised Translation of the Record of Zen Master Jōshū]* (Tokyo: Shunjūsha, 1985).

[9] Matsubara Taidō 松原泰道 is well-known contemporary Zen preacher and
popular author.

[10] Communicated personally on several occasions by Suzuki to the author.

sake of all sentient beings. To watch him in life from day to day was to see an incarnation of the Buddha's teaching of "relentless striving." To this day I am filled with a deep sense of joy for the privilege of having known so singular a human being.

Mahāprajñāpāramitā!

INDEX

Index